BARONY BOOKS

D1678016

DISCOVER THE MAGICK IN YOU

HOW TO INFLUENCE THE COSMIC MIND

Dr Jan de Avalon-Espinosa

BARONY BOOKS

First Edition

Library of Congress Control Number: 2020921321
Copyright © 2020 By Dr. Jan de Avalon-Espinosa
Copyright © 2020 By Baron and Baroness Espinosa BB5063 ESPI

Barony Books website: https://www.baronybooks.com
Cover Design by Dr. Gabriel Foster Espinosa for Barony Books.

Espinosa, Dr. Jan de Avalon-Espinosa
Discover the Magick in You/ By Dr Jan de Avalon-Espinosa

ISBN: 978-1-7353513-4-6 (pbk)
ISBN: 978-1-7353513-5-3 (ebook)

CONTENT

PREFACE

This book will give you a clear insight into influencing the Cosmic Mind. Here we are using a through and concise Cosmic Mind technique as developed by Dr. Jan de Avalon-Espinosa , because we are part of the Universal Consciousness actuality and truth. In here you will discover the Magick that is a latent aspect of your Higher Self, or as I refer to it the Magickal You. People are searching for answers outside of their selves, when all they need do, is to take an inward journey into the invisible realms, the unseen dimensions of existence and bring their hopes, wishes and desires into the physical reality. This is the art of 'Alchemy of Consciousness' by connecting with the Cosmic Mind and becoming Magickal. All human experience has an equivalence and sameness in the spiritual planes, there is no discrimination, no judgment. Everyone has the same opportunity to tap into this higher order of the universe and bring about changes in their world.

The problem has always been, the few that know the truth concerning how Magick really operates, refuse to share this 'simple' knowledge with others. They are selfishly holding onto the greatest secret of the human condition. We are not just mind and body, we are all connected through life-force or the invisible energy of the Cosmic Mind. Some have called this the Universal Mind, Intelligence or Consciousness. It matters not what we title this domain of the Creators Mind, what is important is to understand, that we are all it. We are it, because we are created out of the ONE Unique Mind energy, causing everything to unfold into existence, and become a reality.

Therefore, we all have the innate powers to create, in the same way, as our own mind is connected to the ONE. I believe it is Divine timing that this opportunity to become Magickal is now. You will learn how to rephrase words and sentences, to have a better language pattern that allows you access to your super consciousness, or higher self. I reveal certain exercises to enhance your breathing, your focus and how to create a routine practice, to bring all the ideas together. In Part One we look at becoming confident, in control and empowering yourself for Goal Setting, and how to think differently.

A step by step program, to get you to where you want to be. How to tap into Magickal You, and be a better more charismatic, assertive, and stronger person. In Part Two you will find the alchemy of the elements, and how to understand them. How to utilize these natural forces in nature, as states of consciousness when you create routines, rituals, and practices.

Once you understand that you are not separate from them, you are the elements as the microcosm of the Universe, you will see, feel, and think differently. You will become at-one with the Cosmic Mind.

All things are possible in this Higher Magickal State of Awareness.

INTRODUCTION

I decided to write this book over 20 years ago, but it got shelved. Now and then I was inspired to revisit it, added more information, removed some that did not seem to be useful enough for others to understand. I have been working with Spirit as a child having out of body experiences and 'seeing' energy, orbs, and Light Beings. Magick since a teenager. Countless strange phenomena materialize around me. I had a NEAR DEATH EXPERIENCE when I was seventeen. I have experienced different entities from other dimensionalities and channeled from higher intelligence.

I wanted to share my expertise and ancient knowledge in a modern way. Due to the changes happening in the world, I felt it was time to share this information so that others can experience being Magickal and make changes in their lives. I was taught Magick in many ways, from numerous people, guided in African Magick when I lived in Kenya, and advised by Sangoma in Cape Town South Africa, whilst working on a TV show. So, you could say I have good sound knowledge. Throughout my 30's and 40's, I read all the dusty old magickal books I could find... I practiced different types of consciousness awakening and self-realization methods. I have studied all the consciousness and mind-altering philosophies. I am a very experienced hypnotherapist, NLP and Life Coach, Reiki Master Teacher, Esoteric, Metaphysical, Spiritual and Magick Tutor and much more. I have traveled to many countries and learned so much about their perception on Magick. I am now 70 so you could say I really know what I am talking about. I was extremely fortunate to have brilliant Intellectual Mentors along the way, some were Gurus, Shamans, Rosicrucian's, Golden Dawn, Spiritualists, Theosophists, Free Masons, Magicians, Healers, Mystery School Teachers and NLP experts.

On my life's journey, I have met some very amazing souls, who have shared their knowledge and experiences with me and not always beings of this reality of existence. I want to thank them all.

I especially want to thank my dear friend TFK, for assisting me with insight and content for this book, and for my longtime friend and soul sister Gudi, for supporting me in so many ways and continuously being part of my Magickal journey. We have experienced the results of our 'combined efforts', over the past 20 years, we know what produces great results. We learned the time-wasting systems of endeavor; are not worth the energy you must put into them.

...It is a wonderful thing to change a word to mean more than just the word... All is eternal infinite consciousness, as a reflection of the Creators intelligence, therefore, we communicate multidimensionally, as witness to our own souls' natural existence. When there are no more secrets, opposition, and denial, you are free to function and operate within the great light of absolute supreme consciousness. Your perception of truth alters, by knowing the Creator as the Great Architect of all existence, and his thought alone, brought the Universal Consciousness into being. His existence is time without end, therefore, are we not obliged to embrace the impression, that there is no dissimilarity, but rather there is only eternal order of all existence.

> " Man is all imagination. God is Man and exists in us all and we in him...
> The Eternal Body of Man is the Imagination that is, God, Himself"
> -Blake

The reality is, we are not merely earthly physical creatures who will essentially expire. We are the perpetual Creators and Authors of our own existence and experience, as spirit and matter. Unfortunately, we suffer the experience of obliviousness of our Heavenly and Cosmic nature. Since life itself, gives the impression as a dream or illusion, we continue living this existence as an impermanent life on earth. We can neither perceive nor comprehend our authentic nature as Celestial and Divine or being the absolute equivalent as the nature of creation. We merely continue to endure an existence, which appears to be cut off from this knowledge and wisdom. Initially we are unsighted by an imaginary veiling separating the physical world, from the indistinguishable spiritual domain. Secondly, sacred knowledge, concealed by the nefarious and influential powers that have kept hidden its secrets from man.

1

UNIVERSAL LAW
ORDER AND PRINCIPLE

Some vocabulary, terms, expressions, and definitions are repeated throughout the book intentionally, for the sub-conscious to become accustomed to and acquaint with a new language. Allowing you to familiarize with becoming Magickal.

The Cosmic Mind is that consciousness manifesting you. So then, let us use different words or meanings because language can really get you lost in a maze of analyzing, when analyzing is not necessary, whilst believing is. We function and operate within the entirety of the universe and what it is doing. In the same way that a wave is a function of what the whole ocean is doing, it is 'waving'...Through our own eyes, the universe perceives itself, through our ears it listens. It is 'seeing' and 'hearing'. As we so love... it is 'loving'. Are we but witnesses through whom the universe becomes mindful and deliberately conscious of its own magnificent glory? Therefore, is it not fair to say be minded only to be that which is magnificently glorious.

Universal Laws that never change, we operate and function through them. There are Seven Universal Principles.

1. Mentalism - The Universe is all Mind
2. Cause and Effect - Everything happens according to Law
3. Correspondence - As above so below
4. Polarity - Everything is dual and has poles and opposites
5. Vibration - Nothing is resting everything vibrates
6. Rhythm - Everything flows and has its tides
7. Gender - Everything is both masculine and feminine

Principle-

1. Mentalism and Spirit Consciousness, Cosmic Mind

The source of life is creative consciousness or infinite spirit, immeasurable limitless and everlasting. The Universe as the Cosmic Mind is pure consciousness as Light and the essence spirit/mind ascending above substance, and therefore defined as ruling matter.

2. Causes Effect and Karma

Every single cause has an effect, and each effect has its source. Every action has a design or pattern, intention, and purpose. It is a definite, or specific force that requires similar energy returns to its source, to its origin or designer. The effect equals the cause in attribute, character and quantity or measure. Corresponding creating correspondent, as action equal to reaction.

3. Correspondences and Analogy

As above, so it is below, as below, so it is above. As within, so it is without, as without, so it is within. As in great – so it is in small, as in small, so it is in great. For everything that there is in this world, there exists a correlation, analogy, or similarity on every plane of existence. This is the concurrence and agreement enabling you to realize the great in the small, and the smallest in the greatest. The approach you have to life establishes the way you experience the outside world; the outside world is your mirror or vice versa. When you consciously choose to change, everything around you will also change. What is written on the inside is expressed on the outside. Thoughts becoming experiences and realities, what you change inwardly you express outwardly.

4. Polarity, Resonances and Attraction

Like attracts like and will be enforced and imposed by like, as unlike will repel, resist each other. Your individual and personal behavior determines your personal conditions and the total conditions of your life experience. Positive attracts positivity as light, love, and joy. Bliss attracts bliss, peace more peace, harmony creating more harmony. Negative attracts more negativity, hate attracts hate, sorrow attracts sorrow, addiction attracts addiction, torment creates more torment. If you do not bring an end to negative thoughts and feelings and reverse your path, your negativity as unconstructiveness will increase. This action will inevitably lead you to a downward spiral. Then at a certain point it cannot be reversed, or interrupted or stopped which leads towards   depression, hopelessness despondency, tragedy and ultimately death.

5. Harmonies and Balance

Harmony is the natural flow of life and everything in life strives for harmonization, synchronization, and organization for balance. The stronger and powerful establishes and determines the weaker and makes it equal to itself. Life is melodious and harmonious togetherness, as giving and taking of elements and powers, being effectual and valuable in creation.

6. Rhythms and Vibration

Everything rises and falls, as all things are vibration. Everything flows in and out, as all things have a natural rhythm as the ebb and flow in the tides. Nothing is motionless, fixed, or stationary, everything is moving, and vibrating. Just as a pendulum moves and gathers motion and momentum, it equals the swing to the other side, consequently, the rhythm will match and equalize. Everything has opposing poles as contrasting and dissimilar aspects. Like and unlike are the same. Dissimilarities are the same by their nature.

7. Polarities and Sexuality and Gender

Sexuality manifests equally in everything, both sexual aspects are Oneness, at the same time. Everything has both male and female elements, as One. Sexuality strives for Oneness, yet its reality is Oneness. The unity of sexuality is non-polarization of male and female characteristic. Just as the ocean and the wave are One and cannot therefore be separated or divided. We are male and female at the same time. If you can live your maleness and femaleness aspect equally you are well adjusted and balanced. As the Law of identification or imitation is where one entity assumes the characteristics of another, therefore the more knowledge the first entity has about the second, the superior the imitation. If this produces a good association between both entities, it may almost involve becoming the other entity itself. A transient and provisional identification can be considered as being Divine. Therefore, the Law of Opposites states, that the synthesis on two opposing or conflicting ideas will produce a new or third idea, that will be finding a middle ground and not be a compromise of the original two. This law is used more in mysticism than magick. It allows one to simultaneously hold two opposing ideas without feeling apprehension, foreboding or cognitive discord. The Law of Polarity states anything can be separated into two opposite parts with each part having its own essence. This law is essential to many mystical influences, statements, and arguments. Likewise, it is fundamental in expressing characteristics of objects, such as up and down, right, and left, black, and white etc.

Everything is Connected - We are not separate beings we are all One Energy manifesting into different forms, giving an expression of the creator. The universe is pure consciousness and embodies all that exists. We are the Cosmic Mind in space as consciousness in matter. Consequently, we are creators of our own realities and experiences here in the physical realm. You cannot separate yourself from the conscious energy force that flows through you, around you...
It is the essence of life.

Another Expression of the Universal Laws
http://www.kybalion.org/
The Seven Hermetic Principles. "The Principles of Truth are Seven; he who knows these, understandingly, possesses the Magic Key before whose touch all the Doors of the Temple fly open." The Seven Hermetic Principles, upon which the entire Hermetic Philosophy is based, are as follows:

These Seven Principles will be discussed and explained as we proceed with these lessons. A short explanation of each, however, may as well be given at this point. — The Kybalion.

Universal Connection

Aura, Chakras as Consciousness Cosmic Mind

The Aura is an energy field that surrounds every living thing, this subtle energy field has been acclaimed and recognised by many different cultures for thousands of years. The Aura is the manifestation of our bodies' vibration, the internal electrical system as DNA and atoms. These vibrations become visible via the Aura and emanate through our physical form. They are made up of interconnected electromagnetic waves, that penetrate and extend beyond us several feet, forming an upright ovoid shape. Some say it extends outwardly for 33 feet when we are healthy and fully consciously awakened.

The nature of this electromagnetic energy field is said to reflect the emotional, physical, and mental characteristics of the individual. Overly sensitive individuals can consciously detect this energy that is for most people outside of their awareness. It is this energy that people are unconsciously detecting when they have a 'gut feel' or 'intuition' about someone or something which creates sensitivity and instinct. This electromagnetic energy shows up in the Aura in different frequencies as colours, these colours are the spectrum of Light, and 7 colours are visible and possibly experienced by a clairvoyant or sensitive mystic or psychic. Depending on its 'speed' the colour will vary accordingly, the slowest of these colours is Red the fastest is White. Colour radiates through energy centres known as chakras, and this is a Sanskrit word for 'Wheels 'or 'vortices' that spin. There are seven main chakras, but there are 49 throughout the body, as the harmonics. These chakra centres appear to be the conduit or gateways into the aura field. Chakras are spinning nucleus of conscious energy, interconnecting with the aura and the universal energies and Cosmic Mind. A bridge or conduit, that links us with the Cosmic Mind, the Creator, the Universe, and ourselves.

The word chakra means wheel, disk and spinning vortex that signifies one of seven basic energy centers in the body and is referring to the way energy is moving in circles. They are gateways that relates to the body's energy system, on a physical and metaphysical, incorporeal, or ethereal level. People who are more outgoing have a larger energy field than the average person, or a shy person. People who are despondent, depressed, or unwell will have a diminished energy field and aura. Those auras are dull in color and people who are about to die have the dullest, weakest energy field as it contracts as a diminished energy force. Many people that speak about seeing the aura describe it as a bright rainbow of colors, the spectrum of Light surrounding the body. Our thoughts and feelings as E-motions ultimately have a powerful effect and influence on our physical bodies. It is not possible to separate Mind from Body, they both occupy the same space; however, the Spirit is multidimensional occupying space on various levels of the conscious and unconscious mind. The greater part of us, or the authentic aspect of our being, resides outside of our physical bodies as 'higher consciousness' or higher intelligent thoughts, drawing knowledge and intelligence from the Cosmic Mind. Although we think that our thoughts are only taking up 'space' in our own 'minds' or even our heads...this is not true. Energy moves continuously and unceasingly, just as our thoughts are essentially relentless yet all the same, pure Energy.

To understand the true nature of our Mind-Body-Spirit relationship, we look to the Aura for reactions and answers. If our minds are not focused on positive thoughts, this will cause a reaction in our physical bodies. The same applies with negative thoughts, they eventually become manifest in our material bodies as disharmony and dis-ease. This is basic and fundamental understanding of Cause and effect. Therefore, if your attention is focused on negative, low, and depressing thoughts you will experience chaos, confusion, misery, and illness. However, if you focus on higher positive thoughts, you will attract order, harmony, confidence, and joy, into your reality. You think yourself into your experiences, so be aware of what you want to encounter, what do you want from moment to moment? A healthy and happy mind fashions high spirits besides a healthy body. Ask yourself this, 'do I want a wonderful place for my Spirit/Essence to reside in whilst living in human form, or shall I just not concern myself about the condition of its home?' Negative thoughts will attract others negative thoughts and feelings to your own vibration, you then cause this reality to effect yours. Fear and Love cannot exist in the same space; you cannot experience the sense and feeling of joy and pain, at the same time in the same space. Chaos and Order cannot exist in harmony, one will over-ride the other by the energy and thoughts that you put into it.

Chakras and Auras are expressions of consciousness.

They function as energy expressing itself, they are not physical manifestations. The chakras are more concentrated and denser than auras. They interact with the material body, through two major vehicles or mediums, the endocrine and nervous system. These energy centers or chakras correspond to nerve centers or 'ganglia' branching out from the spinal column. They lie along the center line of the human body and are often displayed in Sanskrit as Lotus flowers, or a series of colored circles or discs. They relate to body functions, the endocrine system, states of consciousness and developmental stages throughout life. They associate to archetypal elements, colors, sounds or vibrations, and more. Together they form a metaphysical principle for wholeness and a template for consciousness and mindfulness transformation. [Alchemy of Consciousness]

The 7 main chakras are the 7 stages in the physical development Every 7-year period we experience a different stage in life and consciousness awareness. This seems to go in line with the idea that there are 7 dimensions as spheres.

- Or your familiarity of being, represents everything it is possible for you to experience. All your perceptions, your senses, and all your potential states of awareness, can be divided into seven modes of classification, and each of these classifications can relate to a specific chakra. Therefore, chakras represent not only particular parts of your physical body, but also particular parts of your consciousness. When you feel anxiety in your consciousness, you feel it in the chakra associated with the part of your consciousness experiencing the stress. Also, in the parts of the physical body related with that chakra. Everything begins its journey into reality from your consciousness, everything that happens in your life, and everything that happens in your body, begins with something transpiring through intention as your thoughts. Your consciousness is connected to your DNA and every cell in your body. Through your consciousness, you can communicate with every organ and every tissue, you can communicate to others, assist in the art of energy healing, or creating a magickal experience. Your Aura will have a certain basic color which means your attention is mainly centered in a particular area of your body. This 'phenomena' is far beyond the comprehension of the 'intelligent 'mind. The intelligent mind must continue to analyze and try to construct some sort of format for self-satisfaction, in knowing 'this really is all that their is'; and therefore, anything bordering on the outside of that understanding or knowing, remains outside of our possibilities. That another reality could not conceivably or possibly exist or be connected to our existence and experience here on this 'earth'.

There is a higher order to the universe, that order can be influenced. The Creator as the Architect of the universe is the great Alchemist and the art of Alchemy, is changing from 'one state' to another. When your conscious mind is foremost, prominent and elevated to your subconscious mind, it is intensifying and escalating your state of understanding, knowing and awareness. These states are subtle, refined and variable vibrations and are beyond our mental perception of awareness . Aligning our own unique frequency to that which reverberates and echoes within the universe.

2

MIND- BODY- SPIRIT

Mind- Body- Spirit

Now, when we speak about mind, body, and spirit, it is as if they are separate from one another, however it is when they function as a single unit that we become magickal. Let us understand the aspects of each element, to be able to develop them and then combine them. This is how we have divided up the body, mind, and brain into a structure for easier understanding. The different aspects and functions of the whole, are presented here so that you can pay attention to individual functions. You can see where your time and attention are being placed, as the starting point for personal awareness and development. The aim is to balance and integrate the different parts, so that you function, and that is where magick begins. Holistically, one being, or being at-one holistically. At-one-ment is to be in-tune or at one with everything or aligned to all there is. The Cosmic Mind.

Mind / Body -For many centuries since Descartes, we have happily divided ourselves up into mind and body as if these were detached from one another. In eastern culture they do not have a 'mind/body' split and now we are discovering that mind and body seem to function together as a single unit. We have created new words like psychoneuroimmunology, to compensate for the fact that we made the division in the first place. So, the following is just a way to think about the different aspects and functions of you. One way of thinking about different aspects of who we are, is to divide up the body and mind, into classifications of the aspects.

The Four Bodies

Before we look at the four bodies let us consider the body as a whole system. We could think of these as the four elements as well. In terms of your physical self rather than the universe or planet earth. After all we are made of all the elements.

Mental Body – Spiritual Body - Emotional Body - Physical Body

Mental Body -This is where we do our thinking analyzing and reasoning. Our Mental Body is the home for our intellect. Someone who spends much of their time here, thinking, analyzing, and evaluating, will seem disconnected and distant. Typically, the eccentric genius. We can consider our mental body to be made up of the pictures and sounds that we make in our heads, and how we talk to ourselves on the inside. These combine to make up our thought processes such as decision-making, reasoning, memory, and imagination. They are also the source of many of our limitations, problems, hang-ups, and doubts. It is the structure of these internal images and sounds that act as the coding for our experiences. It is how we tell one sort of experience from another. It is also where we have our beliefs. There is much debate about the validity of various beliefs, but truly little discussion about what a belief is, and how it functions. At the highest level they are the boundaries of your world. They are an indication of what we have learned. We usually acquire our beliefs by accepting at face value what an authority figure such as our parents or teachers tell us first. Later our beliefs can be conclusions from our own experiences. However, beliefs are made up from the same elements as all our other thoughts. The pictures sound and internal dialogue we create inside our mind. What sets our beliefs apart from other thoughts, is that we will do or not do certain things, based on them. Part of what we are doing in a magickal state, is creating a state of absolute certainty, because one of the things that it does is to provoke action, in the direction of our intention. Why are we always so certain about the things that do not serve us? We already can create magick because certainty is one of the keys. It is just that we are so often certain about things that are not useful. Sometimes even when we know they are not true.

Spiritual Body This is where we are concerned with a connection to a greater awareness. Can appear to be disconnected from reality. There is an understanding that goes beyond words. It is experienced. It cannot be adequately described with words. Your true self, the original self, has been referred to by many names, as divine spark, spirit, essence, holy, and the light body. Every cell in your body is activated by light. These cells are like miniature batteries with north and south poles. Contained within each single cell is the light spectrum a mini rainbow. Light nourishment must be available to replenish the light frequencies, for every cellular unit in the body. Enlightenment means to 'light up '. Non-attachment. When you feel separate to the emotion as if it is not so personal. The dropping of the mind not weighed down with any burdens. There are things to resolve and deal with, but all in good time, which creates a lighter you. Enlighten means to light and that is lighter in you, from higher thoughts and feelings. We say make light of it or heavily burden or weighed down with problems. Spirituality or living in the light is having an awareness of the spirit and living accordingly to one's best ability. No rush, just a constant awareness of connectedness to the universe and your part in it.

Emotional Body We are all emotionally intelligent. What will vary are our attacks of stupidity. Our emotional bodies are made up from our limbic system, nervous system and the chemicals that circulate in our bodies. Our emotions are useful and necessary communications from our body about what is happening to it.

What are emotions? The word emotion is often changed to read 'e-motion' - 'energy in motion.' The actual origin of the word emotion means to 'move out.' It is just a label we attach to a variety of different functions; however, we can define it. The way out is via water and electricity. You are going to scream it out or cry it out. The two great divine forces in basic terms, water and electricity are combined to create the great exodus within. Someone who is 'in their emotional body' is usually overly sensitive to other feelings and easily affected by outside events. How they feel is the most important or over-riding aspect of their lives. "Emotion" is only a label, a convenient way of talking about aspects of the brain and its mind. Psychology textbooks often carve the mind up into functional pieces, such as perception, memory, and emotion. These are useful for organizing information into general areas of research, but do not refer to real functions. The word "perception" describes in a general way what goes on in several specific neural systems. We see, hear, and smell the world with our visual, auditory, and olfactory systems.

Physical Body - When we talk in terms of someone being very much in their Physical Body, what we mean is they are paying attention to physical sensations and reactions. They will often be keen on physical activities, such as sports, dancing, or martial arts. If someone devotes too much time to physical sensations, they may become fitness fanatics, gym, and adrenalin junkies. Or maybe over sexed.

Kinesthetic Description Our physical body is more than just a vehicle for our brain. The energy system that circulates and emanates from our physical body receives and transmits information. In terms of using our physical body to create more powerful and useful states, here is what makes the physical element so important. When we incorporate physical actions along with the visualizations and energy work, it makes the whole act congruent. Our whole body.

Also, when we do something physical first it can then act as a reference for our imagination, when we want to visualize something similar. Balance, breathing and physical movements. For example, if you are imagining bringing energy into yourself, then make the physical actions fit the imagination. Is our physical body designed to survive on this planet and governed by our brain and mind? Or is it just so our brain can experience the planet?

Another point of view-

Your Physical Body: Your physical body is the vessel that your spirituality, emotions, and creativity flow through. The physical, emotional, mental, and spiritual bodies are literal vibrational fields of energy that overlap and affect each other profoundly. The physical body has a great capacity to inform you when something is wrong or right. It can be positively or negatively affected by the foods we eat, the thoughts we think and the emotional state that we reside in at any given moment. Feeling a situation as opposed to thinking about a situation, is the way to effectively use your physical body. This is the ultimate and intended use of the body; the heart will always express itself to you through your feeling/physical body. Learning to "feel" what your body is telling you and responding to those messages is the key to finding harmony and balance. This is the vibrational secret of the Vitruvian Man. You must learn to feel and understand the multitude of energy signatures or messages that your heart is sending through your physical body. In the modern day, people primarily live in their minds separating themselves from their physical body. Our cells energetically remember everything that has ever happened to you, good or bad, and influence the present.

Emotional Body: Your emotional body is the sum of every emotional experience you have ever had and your general concerns pleasures and desires. Did you know that the word emotion means "energy in motion?" Where thoughts and feelings go energy flows. Hurtful experiences throughout life are energetically held as layers of memory (within the subconscious and unconscious mind) within the body that drive day-to-day thoughts and feelings. Therefore, if you are not aware of your inner wounds and have not healed these past wounds, you become a prisoner to the negative energetic influences. Have you ever felt yourself exhibiting unwanted behaviours or reacting in a certain way that did not feel like your true self? These unwanted reactions are the result of emotional wounds, that exist as contracted energy living within you and driving your behaviour. Also residing within the emotional body is love. When something is right or good, we feel the joyous moment, our heart is communicating to us via our positive emotion. This is the desired state of being. Our life's purpose is the fulfilment of the heart. Honouring all that is positive, passionate, joyful, and harmonious leads to this fulfilment. When we heal the layers of emotional wounds, we then move ourselves to a predominate state of joy and love as opposed to experiencing it in fleeting moments.

Mental Body: The mental body is also a powerful, dynamic energy instrument. There are two parts to the mental body: the egoic mind (little mind) and the Divine mind. The egoic mind is a powerful tool for creating a harmonious reality or a reality of suffering. It was not meant to be the driving force of our existence; only a tool to be used to direct and achieve our expanded awareness. When its task of setting an intention or forming a desire is finished, which could be in a few seconds, we should then turn this tool off and return to residing within the feeling body. This gives way to experiencing or residing in Divine mind (I AM PRESENCE). The vibrational experience of Divine mind begins as a subtle calming that deepens into the peace beyond understanding. When existing from Divine mind the constant mental churning is surrendered. However, in modern day, the programming of living within the egoic mind prevents this from happening. It is up to you to choose where you wish to reside – in the churning egoic mind or the peaceful Divine mind.

Spiritual Body: The circle in the Vitruvian Man represents the spiritual body which is the infinite doorway to many high vibrational states of expanded awareness, enlightened awakening, and our mystical self. The secret of the four bodies of existence is that when the physical, mental, and emotional bodies reach a state of harmony and balance, the higher vibration of our spiritual body is activated. Thus, begins the ever-increasing unfoldment of our spiritual nature that begins to open the doorway into enlightened and expanded states of consciousness. These states of expanded consciousness lead to the direct experience of the light of the soul. Throughout the history of humanity, this illuminated state has been lying dormant, waiting to be discovered. It has always been available to mankind. However, for millennium mans' inhumanity to man has perpetuated the prison of pain and suffering.

http://www.soulmerging.com/article/3237-the-four-bodies-of-existance

> *"Through our eyes, the universe is perceiving itself. Through our ears, the universe is listening to its harmonies. We are the witnesses through which the universe becomes conscious of its glory, of its magnificence.""*
> **-Alan Watts**

[There is Extensive Information on this subject in Part Two]

The Elements and Four Bodies

The four elements are a formative composition of conception itself and consequently existing within everything, therefore, considered as the fundamental principle of existence. In the physical world they are the material basis and structure for life and described as the building blocks of the universe. Therefore, this would propose that we could now illustrate the principal nature of everything by reducing it to the four elements. Such is the inspiration it has influenced alchemy, philosophy, magick and modern psychology. So how did the four elements originate, compose, and coordinate themselves, as the original formation and conception was that of pure divine 'Light'?

Science describes them thus-

- Fire- volatile, light, positive electric.
- Air- volatile life energy, positive magnetic.
- Water- condensed life energy, structured energy, and negative energy.
- Earth- mass, matter, dense frozen light, negative magnetic.

I consider there's alternative ways to identify with the four elements and how we operate within these realms. I believe we can experience aspects of ourselves by simply observing the four elements outside in nature and applying certain principles to cause an effect. Therefore, this interconnectedness can be experienced intentionally.

How is this possible? It is possible, when we understand, that we are not separate from the universe, but the microcosmic universe experiencing itself. I see the universe and us as integrated conscious manifestations. The Universal or Cosmic Mind as one, and its parts or aspects of its whole as One. Or-

Fire- The Mental Body it is the nervous system, neurons that fire in your brain, kundalini serpent energy rising through the chakras, to the pineal gland (3rd eye). The eternal creative source of power. The sun, lightening electricity, and flares.
- **Fire**- The Divine Will.

Air- The Spiritual Body it is the intellect and inspiration, communication and information that is carried through your breath and the atmosphere you live in. The essence of life carried in the wind.
- **Air-** Source of Intellect.

Water- The Emotional Body it is the sensations, feelings, emotions carried in your tears, sweat, urine, blood, and internal chemicals. The ocean, rivers, rain, snow, hail, clouds, mist.
- **Water-** Flow of Emotions.

Earth- The Physical Body it is the physical material body, stability, balance, connectedness to gravity and being grounded or earthed. We are made of the same minerals as the planet, we cannot be separated from earth, because we are it.
- **Earth-** Ground your Creative flow.

Therefore, the four elements are pure design and principals of creation, they are metaphorically non- representational, yet they are substance and material. Appropriately reflecting a presence in every dimensionality. Spiritual as essence in nature yet they are manifesting through synthesis. By learning to recognize all aspects within us and express our divine essence, and spiritual qualities through the physical form, our thoughts become our deeds and actions in everyday life.

Earth as the physical life, is our foundation for expressing and realizing ourselves, through our spiritual principles and philosophy, with a purpose to becoming consciously evolved and embrace elevated ideals. What then are we made of? Spiritual Light energy that condenses to a slower vibration called matter, we are by nature, made up of the entire universe, as the same elements and material through the consciousness of the Creator.

There are many ideas and concepts that are connected to the Elements throughout PART TWO; I mention and repeat some of them.

However, basically the purpose is for you to appreciate and recognise the scientific, spiritual, and esoteric ideas, that together they are the underlying principle and foundation to everything in existence. Connecting with the Four Elements as part of you and the Cosmic Mind, allows you to have a sense of what you are made up of and the Universe as a whole.

Your soul is oftentimes a battlefield, upon which your reason and your judgment wage war against your passion and your appetite. Would that I could be the peacemaker in your soul, that I might turn the discord and the rivalry of your elements into oneness and melody. But how shall I, unless you yourselves be also the peacemakers, nay, the lovers of all your elements?"

-Kahlil Gibran, The Prophet

3

THE THREE MINDS

The Three Minds

Here is how we can describe three different functions of the mind. The 3 minds of man or 3 states of consciousness are called -

Conscious - Unconscious (Sub-conscious) -Higher Self (Super-Conscious)

Conscious - To be conscious which is thinking, analyzing making decisions. Conscious comes from con (with) -scious (knowledge, knowing). It is also the same route as the word conscience. What we are aware of right now. Logic reasoning. Conscious is the 'objective' 'I see- I hear- I smell- I touch' it is the force governing the 5 senses. Controls all your voluntary functions and motions. It is the part of the mind that you think and reason with. It controls, to a great extent all your voluntary muscles. It also discriminates between what is right or wrong. Most importantly it is the center of your thoughts on want it is that you want. We are supposed to only be able to focus on or deal with 7 plus or minus 2 chunks of information. This may have been a bit optimistic. Long complicated stuff gets the conscious mind out of the way to quieter the internal chatter. This is the goal of hypnosis, chanting and meditation. This is where we self-analysis. That which was not accessible by ordinary introspection was called the unconscious.

Unconscious (Sub-conscious) - So far scientists have yet to discover any part of the part of the brain that they can call the Unconscious. The closest they have come is to attribute some of its functions to the right hemisphere and we will get to the left/right divide in the next section. The Unconscious is also referred to as the Sub-conscious, which has come to be taken as beneath the conscious mind; hence the metaphor of depth and going under, plus the tendency to draw diagrams with the subconscious beneath the conscious. Subconscious originally meant "not wholly aware," that which is beyond awareness or not fully apparent. The Unconscious mind is a term used by psychoanalysts, and not because there is some disagreement between the functions of the Unconscious and the Subconscious. In the field of personal development, they tend to be used interchangeably. If the conscious mind is that which we are aware of, then the unconscious is that which we are unaware. It does not mean however, that we cannot become aware. In fact, bringing unconscious processes into awareness, and asking better questions of them and their function, can help to move us forward. A popular notion is of learning relates to four stages of awareness. From unconscious incompetence, when you don't know that you don't know; conscious incompetence, where you do know that you don't know; conscious competence, where you do know that you know; unconscious competence. The Unconscious is competent. Period. Your Unconscious keeps you breathing while you are asleep. The sub-conscious mind is the creative faculty within us and creates whatever the conscious mind impresses upon it. The conscious mind is the vehicle of the intellect impresses its ideas and thoughts upon it, which are the expression of belief. Thus, the creation of the sub-conscious is the manifestation of our beliefs.

Beliefs and Values - Sub-conscious is the 'subjective', which occupies the entire body, and keeps everything running perfectly so that you do not have to 'think' to breath. It has unlimited power & controls all the silent and involuntary functions. Blood circulation all secretions and waste plus all cell changes. It heals, repairs and keeping you in good health. It is the 'vital ' link between body-mind and creator. Known as the seat of all memory, every thought or impression is registered and recorded here. Sub- conscious mind takes onboard all what you tell it as 'fact' It is the doorway to the Super-Conscious the power it has is 'unlimited '. You can only communicate to the super-conscious though the sub-conscious. There is no direct access from the conscious mind to the high self. The mind gets in the way. Because the subconscious mind is the creative faculty within us and creates whatever the conscious mind requires; the conscious mind therefore is the vehicle of the intellect; it sets the template of belief upon it and therefore is the expression of your belief. So, the creation of the subconscious self is the manifestation of our beliefs. If you believe that you can create abundance in your life, you are purely creating a template that will crystallize the thought forms to materialize in your reality. If you pay attention to what you don't have, if you pay attention to lack, you create a template to bring into your reality less. When you can understand the simplicity of this, it takes a process of perhaps a few weeks to de-program yourself, de-fragment the old belief system, the old patterns of thought and recreate the new ones.

Higher Conscious / Super Conscious - It is omnipotent and totally 'unlimited' the creative force within. It receives information from your sub-conscious mind, concerning your desires and can attain and fulfil anything for you. It is there to create and do your will. All things are possible if you believe in your Divine Self or Magickal, Higher Self, it only asks of you to have absolute faith. The need for desire is the power behind all action. The ultimate power from which all things precede. It will make known the unknown. There is no direct link between the conscious and the super-conscious. Which is why it makes more sense to place the subconscious between the conscious and super conscious. The only way to access the super conscious is through the subconscious. It is possible to activate the super conscious when the conscious and the unconscious come together.

The Collective Unconscious - Carl Jung created the idea of a "Collective Unconscious" and synchronicity meaningful coincidences. When he spoke about the Higher Self, he used a term more acceptable to the psychologists and psychiatrists that he was presenting his ideas to. He also spoke about the collective unconscious, which he defined as the part of the unconscious, that is common to everyone.

The Extended Mind -The biologist and author Rupert Sheldrake believed that our mind extends beyond the brain. This seems to be an extension of a common phenomenon experienced by amputees. Doctors were puzzled by some of the complaints, by people who had limbs amputated. The mind extends beyond the brain. See phantom limb experiences and Rupert Sheldrake

A Sense of Being Stared At? - We are being stared at, because we are equipped with 360-degree vision in the world of spirit, an unlimited view of everything, all the time. Thoughts are in the ' ethereal ' phantom energy and you are being monitored 24 hours a day, by the universal consciousness or cosmic mind. You are never alone, you're being observed by a higher intelligence and spiritual beings. Your natural perceptions are always outside of you and connect through feelings, or sensation. So, if you begin to feel you are being watched or observed, you probably are. If you get a sensation that there is someone following you, it is 'conscious' energy taking an interest in you, as an energetic being. It is not interested in the physical you, as a John or Mary. It does not have a body to reside in and just curiously investigating any possibilities of incarnating, as a human, or maybe not. Get used to the natural state of the universe and it will respond to you kindly. It is abundantly rich, and full of every conceivable thought; you will get exactly what it is that you think and feel out of the Cosmic Mind.

Your Brain - The brain is the organ with which we think that we think? Here are a few Brian realities., and physical attributes. We have more than one Brain, the solar plexus is often referred to as the second Brain. *I read an article a few years ago and it is said that the 22 letters of the Hebrew alphabet are the same patterns formed by the phosphorene flares, that are fired off in the brain every time you have a thought. Mind blowing concept do not you agree. My thoughts are that this is the origin of ' light language' and that we arrive on earth with it already installed in our computer.* The Brain, its Free Software to get you started. [You can discover more in my other book, 11:11 Language of Light.... the Hidden Matrix .... Cosmic Mind]

Neurology- Neurons that fire together, wire together. Creating pathways of neurons in the mind. How do we use this? By doing something that creates new connections between the neurons. It is not the number of neurons, but the amount of connections between them.

Chemistry - Experiments on the brain have involved Anatomy of the brain and then some specific organs within it and their function, in relation to spiritual practice. What chemicals are released, certain chemicals are released that cause certain emotions etc. this chemistry extends beyond the physical brain and flows throughout the body, -by Candice Pert Molecules of Emotions. These chemicals are released into our aura via breath, sweat and tears

Anatomy - Investigating the brain has often been conducted by studying people who have had traumas to their brains and are unable to perform certain functions. At a basic level.

Brainwave Frequencies - (Healing states are the ability to have two or three states of consciousness, all running at the same time)

- Alpha, Delta, Beta, Theta
- Alpha7-13 hertz (cycles per second) Restful relaxing state
- Delta1.5-5 hertz the sleeping state
- Beta13-30 hertz the waking state
- Theta4-7 hertz Deep state of relaxation

Left Brain / Right Brain - Here is a way to easily divide the brain based on its anatomy. The brain is divided physically down the central axis. The two halves connected by a bundle of nerves called the Corpus Callosum. Damage to the brain sides. People with damage to the right side can remain positive and unmoved by their circumstances. Left side damaged can be very miserable. Each half has been assigned a certain role, with the left side being called logical and the right side creative. As convenient as this might be it is over simplistic, and the function of the brain is more holistic. However, let us look at how these two halves have been assigned their different roles. Nothing about the brain is quite so straightforward. Ultimately it is how the brain works that counts. Some people have decided that since the right brain is the source of our creativity etc., that it is the unconscious. Again, this is just another way of talking about things we are not sure about. The idea of using some physical exercises and movements, to get both sides of the brain working together, is an ancient one the oldest way known to bring together the two sides of the brain is to dance. We need only look at the American Indians, there are many sacred dances still used today. The labyrinth walk is another great way to get both sides of the brain coordinating. Add a chant and you are in the perfect state to communicate with a higher intelligence. An ancient method of bringing the two hemispheres of the brain together, is embedded very deeply into our unconscious mind. Focusing on movements and adding singing or chanting, create the perfect state for higher communication. A more modern approach is to cross hands in front of your face and with two fingers of each hand press firmly between the hairline and eyebrows for a few moments. In doing this, you will simply freshen up the circuits of the neuro vascular system. Giving the brain a boost or energy surge.

Left Brain -Uses logic, detail oriented, Facts rule, words, and language present and past, math and science, comprehends, knowing acknowledges, order, pattern perception Knows object name, Reality based, forms strategies, practical structure.

Right Brain - Uses feeling, intuition, "big picture" oriented Imagination rules, Symbols and Images present and future, philosophy and religion can "get it" (i.e. meaning), believes appreciates Spatial perception, knows object function, fantasy based, presents possibilities, Impetuous, risk taking.

4

PSYCHIC ATTACK AND DEFENCE

Psychic Attack and Defence

You can attach the thoughts and feelings of the Four Elements to your Attack or Defence simply by moving into that state first, before you do anything else. It is always about the state you are in that determines the outcome. There is extensive information on this subject in Part Two.

Psychic Attack - One way of defining psychic attack, is to consider it negative psychic influence, that includes an intention to cause harm. However, we can also end up 'attacking' ourselves, through our habits and thinking, although there is no intention to do so. It is often just the way things are as far as we are concerned. The classic definition of psychic attack is voodoo and the evil eye. Even though the original intention of voodoo was healing, it also included causing harm through the same process of projecting thought or energy towards the recipient. As well as that, I want to add another distinction, because it happens so often. This is when someone is attacking your psyche, you are thinking, thereby, usually confusing you and trying to manipulate you. Depending on how we define psychic attack, we can come up with all sorts of things that we could consider to be attacks. The simplest distinction to make is that it is not a physical or verbal attack. It does not happen directly to you, but you do feel the consequences of it. At the simplest level, someone who is in a bad mood and insists that you join them in their misery. They do not actually have to say anything to you. They are the kind of person who can suck all the joy out of the room, when they enter. We will deal with these three different forms of psychic attack. You can have an effect on yourself through your own negative thinking and habits; other people can get you to think differently and question your own beliefs, place doubt etc.; they can also project bad vibes to you without any form of contact.

- Your own negative thoughts.
- Attacking you with their negative thoughts.
- Attacking your psyche.

You can give yourself such a hard time. Talking to yourself, guilt, and worry. Self-talk and internal dialogue the inner chatterbox. There is usually no intention to harm, which just happens to be the result it disrupts your clear thinking. Here the trick is disassociating, so that you can re-evaluate, then to add some strategies around that. Of course, that is what they would do given the circumstances etc.

Stopping Your Internal Dialogue - Tell it-

- Stop it. Go to your room.
- Be quiet or shut up and be firm with it.
- Imagine you are on the phone and cannot be interrupted, this is an especially important phone call.
- No, not now too busy.
- Treat it like a naughty child and be firm.
- No, you are not getting your own way.
- Get it out of your head somehow-
- Write a letter.
- Make some physical representation, of what it is that is bothering you.
- To create magick, you must first give action in the physical world.
- Getting rid of stuff as well as attracting it.

If you are full to the brim with old unwanted information in your internal filing system, make room for new information. Send unwanted clutter to the 'trash bin' or 'delete' all unnecessary rubbish. For fresh brilliant (bright) ideas to develop, they require growing space and need to be watered. Get rid of the 'weeds' so that the 'seeds' (thoughts) can grow and flower without being strangled by unwanted memories thoughts and feelings.

Attacking Your Thoughts - Some people just want you to join them in their misery. It is part of how they relate to others. They are sometimes known as 'psychic vampires' that drain your energy from you.

Negative thoughts from others - When someone is directing negative thoughts towards you or wishing you harm. The attack may be sent at a distance, by constant powerful undesirable, destructive or unkind thoughts directed at you. People plotting against you, or someone wanting something from you, or they plan to disrupt your life. They are projecting their selfish and greedy thoughts towards you. A person whose intent is distracting you, or your partner and causing deliberate harm. Someone jealous or envious of what you have, your home, children, business, or partner, also achievements.

Other ways to attack through direct approach, by influencing your pattern of thought, to cause you to change your mind and even draw energy from you, to weaken you physically and mentally. Do not become a clone of your partner, let him or her be who they are, and you be you. Mind games can be very damaging and dangerous, in any relationship. No one ever wins, you end up trying to 'outthink' and 'outsmart' each other, what a waste of time and energy. Much better to admit to the way things are and project thoughts to change the way you feel, and perhaps see the problem from his or her perspective. Not easy but doable. Start creating a more satisfying experience for yourself, and in that way, you will automatically influence your partner.

Confusion - One of the hallmarks of confidence tricksters and people who are manipulative, is that they communicate in such a way to confuse you; so that they can get you to agree to something you wouldn't normally otherwise. Not that everyone who confuses is out to trick or manipulate you, but this is something worth understanding and remembering. Whenever someone is in a state of confusion, it can be that uncomfortable they want to do something, to get out of that state. They will tend to do or think the first thing that makes sense to them, in the context. This is a way that someone can get you to agree to something, that you would not have agreed to if you hadn't been confused in the first place. Beware! Whenever you feel confused or overloaded with information, you need to take time out, clear your head. Anyone who puts pressure on you to decide, or agree to something under these circumstances, is not doing you any favours. The way you can do this, is to place your attention on something you are certain about. Get your attention back outside yourself. Clear your mind. If you don't clear your head and make good a decision, then once they have got you to agree to something, then they can use the phrase "but you said..." and you'll feel obliged to be consistent, with your previous agreement. This is one of the techniques used by salesmen when getting you to sign contracts etc. In Contract Law any agreement extracted under duress, can be considered null and void. I am not giving you legal advice here, but there is a precedent that you can use to make a deal with yourself, so that you cannot be manipulated through guilt and the consistency principle.

Incongruence - When someone's words and deeds match 100%, then we can call this congruence and maybe even describe that person as having integrity if we like their values. However, on a more basic level when you are communicating with someone congruence becomes important. When what they say and what they do, do not match. Even in the same sentence someone can agree with you and be shaking their head 'No'. Psychologists have concluded that communication consists of what we say, how we say it and what we do. They have examined our response to incongruent messages, when what we say does not match how we say it. They discovered that we tend to believe, or give more credibility to, the non-verbal part of the message. They even came up with some statistics that people could quote regarding exactly what percentage, of our communication is made up by the words we speak, the tonality we use and all the other non-verbal behaviour we express. However, this assumes that the non-verbal part of our behaviour is delivering only one message. When someone sends us conflicting messages and we do not have a way of dealing with it, we can end up feeling uneasy about it without knowing why. Once you can detect it you just need to plant a label on it and label it incongruent, so you do not have to take it on board. They use words, vocal qualities, and body language.

Overcompensating

Sometimes when we feel down or sad, we try to 'put on a brave face.' There is something about how we behave when we are doing that, which is not congruent. It is not that we are sending mixed signals, or our true feelings are showing through, it is that our behavior can appear to be too much for the context. We are unable to gauge how happy we should pretend to be to compensate for our actual feelings. It is as if we feel we need to compensate for those negative feelings, by behaving in a manner that we would not normally consider.

Exaggerative, over emphasizing, too dramatic too loud, protesting.

When we are feeling a certain way and want to appear to be the opposite, we tend to amplify our behavior. But because we are feeling low, let us say it is difficult to gauge our behavior and we tend to over-compensate. Beware someone who over-states his or her case.

There is a great quote from Looking After Number One by J Ringer. He states the protesting lady from Hamlet or Mac Beth. The protesting lady, "ma lady doth protest, too much me thinks" So, if someone is over the top, and you buy into that behavior. You are actually better off assuming the opposite. Information is eagerly volunteered without any prompting or for any apparent reason. Beware! Ignore all neurotic remarks and behavior of ordinary people. Ignore all remarks and behavior of neurotic people. Let them go out of your life. This is the major lesson for many of us. The ability to just let go and then move on. Resist the temptation to tell others and get caught up in their world of nonsense. Do not do things to get back at them. If you attempt to carry on a relationship with someone who is crazy, given enough time, they can convince you, that you are the one who is crazy.

Projection - When someone cannot accept a part of themselves, they can project that behaviour onto others. On a normal level, this seems to be a means of explaining the concept that relationships can act as mirrors. We see in our partners, that which we can learn about ourselves. If you want a quick way to highlight your faults and shortcomings, then have a relationship. Now, if we have a deep-seated belief that we don't like ourselves, or there are parts of our personality we are unable to accept, we will have the feeling associated with it, but because we are disconnected from its true source that feeling gets projected onto others. In other words, we see in others the behaviour we do not like in ourselves. When you are on the receiving end of what appear to be unfounded accusations this may be the source.

For example, we can be attacked when we are vulnerable, ill, or sensitive emotionally. Sometimes you are not in awareness until the situation comes upon you suddenly. You can be in a joyous situation someone enters your space in a state of anger or fear. Information travels in the fluidic essence, in the atmosphere. Any focused intention, to do well, or harm moves in the same way. It is transmitted through the brain and moves via the aura / chakra system into the electro-grid, magnetic field, or what I call the ultra-net. When a thought begins to expand, with the energy put to it, there is not necessarily a direction until it is given sense or feeling added to it. Now it can have a direction in which to move towards and dependent on the feeling, good bad or ugly. Loving or hating...healing. Without sense of feeling attached it is harmless and noninvasive to another's field of perception. However, add a powerful feeling to that thought and you get something quite different. It has a life of its own and to realize its own expression in the vast sea of consciousness. Now it can move towards its target to begin a ' nesting process ' in that person's electro-magnetic field and awareness. When a person thinks that someone does not like them, they are usually correct at a very deep level of awareness and no words are needed to express it...just a feeling.

Have you ever experienced this? Walked into a room and felt unwelcome, talked about, uncomfortable, it is all in the air. You have been talked about and it lingers for you to step into. Horrible. You could 'cut the air with a knife'. Perhaps the expression can make 'sense' now and you may begin to understand why a knife or sword in magick represents air. To have awareness at an unconscious level would mean that your higher self would take care of any unwanted vibes, waves and negative energy that could possibly cause a disturbance in your frequency. Daily I remind myself that my higher self-will guard me from any unwanted disruptions from anyone thinking ill, or unkind thoughts, and not just about me but all people. My intention is to remain at a level of awareness on another frequency, so that I do not attract any negative thought forms into my field of energy.

Negative Energy -Some people have a way of dealing with their issues around energy that latches onto other people and drains them of theirs. Energetic vampires. I am positive you have met some. They always leave you feeling 'drained', exhausted and confused.
Be aware that not everyone in life will like you. Some will deliberately cause you harm one way or the other, it is just the way they function, on a lower level or reality.

Psychic Self-Defense - When something happens in our lives that we have a strong reaction to we tend to remember the event and our response as one unit. So, when we think about what happened we have the same emotional response to it. You could say that our mood does not just colour our world it determines it. To get another perspective on these memories, it can be useful to separate the two again, so that we can step back from it and re-evaluate. Learning the art of psychic defence can help you survive the wrath of others that are determined to create havoc in your life, from the unseen world. There are always those out there who seek the opportunity to disrupt or destroy, the good that others have worked for. Being in a strong position to defend yourself and your friends and family will place you in a winning position. Attention to your attitude towards what may be happening and using your skills to prevent those unwanted setbacks.

You can use all the techniques from the 'element energies' to stand firm, energize and take charge of your emotions. Here are some more you can add. The simplest form of protecting your energy in the presence of someone, is to place your hand over your solar plexus and turn slightly at an angle. Imagine letting any negative energy sail past you. Here are another couple of things, that you can do to protect yourself. First, go in a bubble of sacred energy and feel safe there, or look through the eyes of a hero. Being one step ahead of the crowd will place you in a prime position for success. Simple yet powerful techniques that repel attack from others and keep you safe in your bubble of energy. Write the name of a person or event, on the shell of an egg. Then crack it open, and as you whisk it up say the words "I shall consume you", see your breath going into it. Add some milk to represent the essence of your spirit. Make scrambled eggs with it, then as you eat it think about the idea of being an enormous entity, consuming a small annoying spirit.

They will never bother you again.

Your Secret Mantra -This works when someone is trying to plant ideas in your head or get you to agree to something. By simply repeating "No" to yourself, inside your head, or something that is not what they want you to believe, or take on board, you can counter their intention. Make sure your voice on the inside has the right tone to it. Be firm with your voice. Like a boss or sergeant major, in the army. You can think of what they are trying to do as firing neurons in a certain direction. What you are doing is firing your own neurons back at them, to neutralize their attack. Imagine it like a video game. This also works when an unwelcome idea or thought keeps popping into your mind. However, for this to work you must do it every time it happens. Do not let one pass by. The idea is to cut it off quickly. Zap it with your own neurons.

Think Only Positive Thoughts - Mental house clearing, or mind spring clean. Stop, take 2 breaths because it is the second one that releases the negative energy. As you do this you need to picture an empty room with the door and window open and the wind whooshing around. Or a yard filled with fallen leaves and the wind blowing and scattering them.
Or blow a balloon up in your mind and let it burst.

Cartoon Time - Take control of the representation in some way. I remember once that someone kept popping into my mind and interrupting me. I could not get them out of my head, so I turned them into a cartoon, and shrunk them to a tiny size. However, it turned out that I could still hear them. So, I put them into a glass jar. When I thought about this person I did not get dragged into an argument or start going over old ground of negative thinking.

When you are doing this, you are taking control of the representation and this alone will change how you feel and react. Not only does it help disconnect your feelings from a situation, but by having some fun with it you can laugh at it.

Attention Back Outside - Get out of confusion. Get your attention outside of yourself to something in your environment that you do understand. Turn around, clap or stamp your feet. Re-connect to your body and look at the ground and take a deep breath in through your nose and exhale through your mouth, as you breathe out look up at the sky and imagine blowing clouds away.

Really? -Do not buy into it. Once you have your defence in place. "Really?" "Does it?" "Is it?" Get curious about what they are saying without buying in to it. If you answer the questions that are put to you, you have accepted the presuppositions behind the question or statement. You can say- What makes you think that? How long have you been thinking like that? When you feel like you are being unjustly attacked decline to take it on board by reflecting it back. If they are operating from a position of projection. This is a great metaphor, vampires cannot see their own reflection, and they cannot stand bright light. Being examined, put under the spotlight. Act as a mirror. To implement this at an energetic and psychic level, just imagine you are standing behind a tall 2-way mirror, you are safe, and the negative energy is reflecting back to the person. Chuckle to yourself, as you do this, for this is a great idea.

Create a Protective Bubble - One of the most effective methods of protecting yourself is to create a bubble of energy around you.

To prepare for this just start breathing in rhythm. Inhale to the count of 1-2-3-4 and exhale out to the count of 1-2-3-4-5-6-7. Imagine you are breathing in colors like inhaling the rainbow. As you breathe in begin to get stronger as you fill yourself with colors. Then after a few moments as you exhale, imagine being inside a large bubble. Blowing a bubble, when it is fully blown about 8 feet tall, imagine you are inside it. And it will protect you because nothing can penetrate.

When this type of experience enters your life do this- Concept and Process.

Bottomless Pit - Quick Fix

If you are feeling

- Depressed

- Afraid

- Stuck

- Unlucky
- Rejected
- Going in circles

You are thinking

- How did I get here?
- Why me?
- It's all my fault
- There is nothing I can do.
- Feel sorry for your self
- Blame others

STOP! This is what you can do right now!

What are your resources and what can I do?

- This is where I am at right now
- What do I need to do?
- What resources have I got
- I can change things around
- Create better thoughts
- Feel good about your self
- New belief system
- Positive Feelings
- Controlled Emotions
- Be Confident
- Plan of Action

What you need to do?

- It is only temporary
- Everything is changing moment to moment
- Believe in yourself
- Tap into good, happy, and positive memories

- Tap into confident feelings

- Magical moments that make you smile

- Tell yourself funny stories

- Watch a comedy film

- Laugh at yourself and others

Your Resources are inside of you

- Change State

- Clear thinking

- Be positive and certain

- Take control regain your own power

- Feel a little daring and courageous

- Act do something that makes a statement that you are serious.

Remember you can change your reality with powerful structured thoughts and feelings.

5

SPIRIT OF HIGHER CONSCIOUSNESS

Spirit of Higher Consciousness

Acknowledged and regarded as the Holy Guardian Angel, Higher Self, Divine Self, but I prefer to name this entity as Cosmic Self. Magickal You.

The soul possesses a great influence called love, which is the assimilation of 'the one'. The one living force within the soul is creation of life itself. Celestial supremacy is concealed within the body of man. Heavenly, immortal, and divine is thus, the very spirit of man.

Did you not know that you are a spiritual being having a human experience? In all traditions there are beings with a consciousness greater than our own. In the west we call this consciousness an angel. The soul's language and expression are love, and within the matrix of the essence lays all opportunity of truth. Whereas the language of the intellect has the capacity for deception, every spoken word creates endless possibilities, and nothing existing without cause. The absence of knowledge of cause can easily be a factor to our lack of understanding our problems. There are many references to guardian angels and what role they play in the scheme of things. But who is 'The Holy Guardian Angel'? The spirit of Higher/Super Consciousness. An inner entity that experiences insights and seen as some sort of spirit guide?

" The term Holy Guardian Angel was possibly coined either by Abraham of Wurzburg, a French Cabalist who wrote a book on ceremonial magick during the 15th century or Samuel Liddell MacGregor Mathers, the founder of the Hermetic Order of the Golden Dawn, who later translated this manuscript and elaborated on this earlier work, giving it extensive magical notes, but the original concept goes back to the Zoroastrian Arda Fravaš ('Holy Guardian Angels').[citation needed] In Mathers' publication of The Book of the Sacred Magic of Abramelin the Mage, he writes:

There are theories of the Magickal You, being in some way associated with the divine manifest within humanity, as an 'internal entity.' Whatever the Magickal You fundamentally is, it does give the impression of being ever vigilant, perceptive of our interests and proficient to present insights. Successful work with the Magickal You, is not merely discovering one's own talents and potentiality, but is somewhat more ethereal and yet personally significant.

Your superior consciousness, in *'space' as 'space'* itself is all consciousness.

Plato - remarked, "we should think of the most authoritative part of our soul as a guardian spirit given by god which lifts us from earth towards our home in heaven."

Magicians have said the same thing about the Magick You. It is not a separate entity. So, what purpose does it serve? There are several different definitions; All of these are references to the Magickal You - Super Conscious, Divine Self, Universal Mind, Holy Guardian Angel, Higher Being, Higher Self, God Self, and Inner Self. Or even the Fairy God Mother or Genii. Old Fairy Tales had a unique way of letting us know about our Magickal, Higher Self. It is the observer within that watches and monitors all your actions. It's non-judgmental and devoid of emotional attachment to whatever your choices may be. It is also there to serve you. Yes, did you get it? Serve you! To access that state, you must begin by eliminating negative thoughts and feelings of failure and doubt. Forgive yourself for poor choices and decisions and forgive others for theirs. Once you have achieved this state you are easily able to begin the process of communicating. Once you are communicating consciously things change forever.

You Need To- Create a bigger stronger signal from your instincts. Popular psychology has attributed different functions to different hemispheres of the brain. The idea is that the right side is the source of intuition and creativity while the left side is the source of logic and reasoning. Sometimes these have been extended to mean that the left side is the sub-conscious, but this is just a way of talking about different aspects of the mind. It is more interesting to experience what happens when both sides of the brain are activated at the same time. When the whole brain is activated then you have access to the super-conscious or the higher intelligence.

Left Brain – logic, sequencing, linear thinking, mathematics, facts, thinking in words.

Right Brain – imagination, holistic thinking, intuition, arts, rhythm, nonverbal cues, feelings visualization, daydreaming.

You Need To - Communicate to others and get messages across. The way you connect to your Magickal You is by activating all aspects of your brain and mind. As previously mentioned, there are three minds, the conscious, sub-conscious and super-conscious. In simple terms, getting the everyday chatter of the conscious mind out of the way and activating both sides of the brain can give you access to your higher self and you are easily able to send messages through this method of thought transference.

You Will- Feel more connected to source/creator. The moment you close your eyes and shut out the natural light, your own resources automatically kicks in for you to communicate to your creator, through the vehicle or medium as Magickal You via the 3rd eye or the 'pineal gland'. Realities are constantly cascading down through space and time, and as they fall, they forget the previous level of existence. You enter the possibilities of space and consciousness each time you shut down to meditate. It is in this state, you begin the process remembering all aspects of your-self, or all the many parts of you that were forgotten. The divine spark of your creator reveals itself to you.

You Will - Become more self-aware through feeling and paying attention to physiological signals and your inner voice-It is different for everyone. You will know Magickal You is communicating to you by the feelings as they move through the body ending up as the goose bumps, shivers, shakes or something else. In general, most people have a sensation of rain falling over them and some have tingling others have experienced hairs standing on end. These sensations may last a few moments sometimes longer and will end with the feeling of inner peace, joy, and bliss.

Spirit of Super Consciousness or Magickal You

Magickal You - It is often represented in fairy tales as the genii in the lamp or bottle or the 'fairy god mother'. Who we call to, or wish for, that assists us in times of need or sorrow? However very few people realize that we can communicate with this entity as an aspect of ourselves to attract and manifest things in our life. The Magickal You or Higher Self is not actually 'higher' than you are rather it is the forgotten level of awareness.

Your Superior Self - When you want to approach the great powers within and bring together these invisible forces to the visible and tangible world of your reality, it is then that you achieve your potential. Everything is possible in the universe. Yet the misunderstanding blinds us still? That we must see something to believe in it, when faith is all that is required of us. Electricity was invisible and existed before it was discovered too. Dark becomes Light yet they both exist.

You have gone through life only knowing the ordinary self. Being unaware a Magickal Self exists. Thinking that only certain people are magical. Believing humans have no special powers. Thinking that you cannot attract the right people, love and romance, wealth, and a better career. Convinced you are dull and uninteresting, unable to be in control powerless and mundane. Lack confidence and have low esteem. The Magickal You is a latent characteristic and aspect of you, expressing itself as a superior intelligence. Renowned magicians have all said the same thing about Magickal You. It is not a separate entity.

Plato remarked, "we should think of the most authoritative part of our soul as a guardian spirit given by God which lifts us from Earth towards our home in Heaven." Meaning from material physical to our origin as spirit.

The Bible states, that God said, he would give us a guardian throughout our journey on the planet but what most of us have not realized is that the guardian was actually our higher self, the Angelic self. This is the direct link between man and God and the connection was given so that we would always remain in God's presence. And God would remain in ours as the source of all life. It is your consciousness that existed before you were born in the material world and will continue existence once you die. Remember the quote 'I am the alpha and the omega,' the beginning and the end. The name 'Holy Guardian Angel' does sound somewhat pompous and grand, I much prefer Magickal You. What you call this force/entity does not really matter. In fact, one of the biggest pitfalls in magickal work is taking yourself too seriously, so if you can think of a more pompous sounding title to remind you of that pitfall then be as creative as you like. Generally, there appear to be three theories about Magickal You that can be thought of as psychological processes or concepts, external entities, internal entities. Each theory has its merits; however, experience does not need a theory.

Here is what Aleister Crowley had to say about The Magickal You /Holy Guardian

> "Let me declare this Work under this title: 'The obtaining of the Knowledge and Conversation of the Holy Guardian Angel, because the theory implied in these words is so patently absurd that only simpletons would waste much time in analyzing it. It would be accepted as only a convention, and no one would incur the grave danger of building a philosophical system upon it"

With this understanding, we may rehabilitate the Hebrew system of invocations. The mind is the great enemy; so, by invoking enthusiastically a person whom we know not to exist, we are rebuking that mind. In simple terms, getting the everyday chatter of the conscious mind out of the way and activating both sides of the brain can give you access to your Higher Self or Magickal You.

Connecting to Magickal You - Entering the inner dialogue that has endless and constant potentiality, of all possibilities. Exercises to create an identity separate from your ordinary self, so that you have a new distinctive aspect free from everyday clutter and issues to create your magick.

How do you communicate? Basically, you just need to get out of your own way. One of the things that prevent us from being aware of the signs and signals from our Magickal You, is that we are just too busy doing everyday things, like worrying about money, rushing around at work, getting the shopping and falling in and out of love. Activating your Magickal You is not a process of adding. It is a process of stripping away.

There is an amazingly simple yet profound way to communicate, in doing so this allows you to have a direct line to your creator. Also connecting to your Magickal You, allows you to communicate very easily with the spirit realm. After all, you are partly a Celestial being. It is as if we have three separate minds: the conscious, the unconscious and the Magickal You. Although they are spoken of as if they were separate parts, I believe they are more accurately thought of as different functions of the whole mind/brain. It appears that there is no direct link from the conscious mind to the Magickal You. It is only through our unconscious mind, that we can connect to it.

The unconscious, or sub-conscious mind is your internal servant and computer and knows no difference between good and bad, it just receives information and accepts it. It understands in symbols and numbers. Since symbols and numbers can communicate complex ideas and associations, very quickly and simply, the use of symbols is one of the most powerful aspects of magick. The greatest key to manifesting your desires is to believe in your own power. Unfortunately, as humans many of us rely solely on the 'left brain,' which is the logical and scientific side, and in general the more dominate. However, the 'right brain' is by far the most powerful as it is entirely your imaginative and intuitive side. It is the magickal creative side of your brain. Again, the notion of 'right brain' and 'left brain' are ways of talking about functions of the whole brain. I do not believe that these functions exist exclusively in separate sides of the brain. There is a lot of emphasis in personal development and New Age books and courses on learning to use the 'right side' of your brain, but this is just a way of talking.

Importantly, I would like to mention that loving you, all the aspects of you would put you in the correct state to communicate with your Magickal You. In a simple language, you need to fall in love with the essence of YOU.

Preparation to Connect
More on this Later

First, it is paramount to prepare yourself mentally beforehand simply by moving away from self-identity and the perceptions of the persona or individual. Letting go of individuality, allows the true self an achievable experience. You will learn how to do this by clearing your mind of any internal clutter as previously mentioned. Also, before any session I would suggest that you have a bath or a shower and use frankincense. If you are taking a bath, submerge yourself completely under the water, you can also add lots of Epsom salt to the water, this will help freshen up your aura. After a bath or after a shower you can even use salt, preferably sea salt and rub it on your skin, and leave it on your skin just for a few moments and just brush it off. This also will act as cleansing your aura. Put on very loose fresh clothes. They ought to feel amazingly comfortable and if you always use the same outfit then it will only be associated to the magick and putting it on becomes part of the change of state that you need.

Experience Connecting to 'Magickal You' - When I tap into it there are certain physical sensations and visualizations that accompany that state of awareness. I am going to describe them below, but you may have a different sequence of sensations, or a different set altogether. First, I see a bright light in my mind, and I have inner active sensations of feeling excited in the solar plexus. You might describe it as 'butterflies in the stomach. Then I get rush of energy that moves all through my body. Next on the outside it feels as though something is gently sweeping across the top of my head, as if I am being gently stroked on my hair, it gets stronger and stronger until I can feel electricity on top of my head. In Hawaiian Huna they call this "The Rain of Blessings." Imagine a fine mist falling on your head, or electricity in your hair. I get a feeling like cobwebs falling over my body, a tickling sensation on my skin. I can get goose bumps and shivery. I can get ridiculously hot a flush go through my body; my lips begin to tingle, eyelids flutter and an incredible power surge of electricity from base zone/chakra upwards through my spine. It is very sensual and remarkably like an orgasm. It is a feeling of total bliss and joy. I know I am at one with the universe. This is when I know that a message is coming through.

How will you know if you have connected to your Magickal you? You might have a similar experience or one that is unique to you. You will notice some specific sensation that lets you know that something different is happening. In general, most people have a sensation of rain falling over them and some have tingling others have experienced goose bumps and hairs standing on end. These sensations may last a few moments, sometimes longer and will end with the feeling of bliss. You may experience a deep and profound emotional surge. It could be making you very tearful or even an overwhelming feeling of absolute joyousness. On other occasions a strange sensation in the solar plexus, not unlike nervous anxiety, like a blind date, interview or falling in love.

When I tap into that state for a healing session or to give an angel reading to someone, I can connect with them and they begin to have a similar set of sensations that I am picking up.

There have been many different experiences when people have communicated with their Magickal You, I am only giving you a few. You will soon recognize the message or reply from Magickal You, it will be unlike any other sensation that you previously felt. Some even hear ringing or humming sounds or the feeling of being tapped on the head or air being blown on their face. It is different for everyone. You will know it is communicating to you by the feelings, as they move through the body ending up as the goose bumps, shivers, shakes or something else.

6

MAGICK BEGINS IN THE MIND

Magick Begins in the Mind

Changing language patterns is all part of the techniques. You are actually heading in a new direction by using well thought out' language patterns' or at least only for programming the mind 'to set the desire or intent', that you want to attract to yourself. That desire or intent could mean, achieving your goals, attracting more business, changing direction, or solving a problem. You can achieve your goals and control yourself in almost any given situation, by using these simple techniques. Using the principles of magick can provide time and space for the unconscious mind to 'alter' or 'change state', or make necessary changes in the pattern of thinking, that is fixed in the memory. These patterns create old 'habits' or the way that we individualize or collectively perceive other ideas of 'something'. Sometimes the 'something' is inexplicable, or unexplainable but that does not mean it isn't 'real'. It is 'real' enough, simply because someone has witnessed it. But not necessarily possible to explain its feasibility and authenticity. Therefore, an explanation of what he or she has seen or felt, when witnessing the event, seems to the non-observer to be 'unbelievable' or 'too farfetched' Hence, so many unexplained 'strange' phenomena, which in point of fact could be arguably categorized as 'the norm'.

Mind Mastering Techniques - Mind Mastering is simply modern magickal techniques that will enhance concentration, build confidence, help focussing, and help you to easily 'change state' and see things more clearly and vividly. In that 'magickal state' you are more likely to be able to attract the things that you want and desire, achieve your goals and become more creative and attractive, magnetic, and charismatic. In this 'magickal state' and 'higher level' of awareness, you can 'see' and 'image' solutions to problems, think more positively, act on 'gut feelings' and have an all-round 'feel good factor'. Positive thoughts create actions. These simple yet profound techniques be a 'modern' approach to 'old magick' and this modern approach works, because it has been tried and tested over the years.

"I was a student of 'old magick' at a young age and also in later years in Africa, I was very privileged to be 'mentored' and 'guided' by an old Juju man or Witch Doctor, so you could say I have developed my own kind of magick by blending them together"

The structure of magick never changes in its nature. Why? Because it is nature itself and we are not separate or distant, nonetheless, we are part of its function and routine. When we realize where we 'fit' into the picture, you could say it is a 'light-bulb' moment, a revelation and things are never the same again.

Create Magickal States - It is the consensus that Magick must remain mysteriously out of reach for us, with the exception given only to the dedicated Magician and his apprentice. But I intend to reveal ancient knowledge in a practical up-to-date way, so that you can get results right away and not have to wait for years, doing the same old rituals and using all the nonsense unnecessary paraphernalia.

The art of magick is practiced through an intermediary called 'ritual', you could easily call it a 'routine', 'practice' or 'exercise' if you want to give it a more modern approach. Magick is a conceptual system accentuating man's capacity to assert influence and control of the natural world, through mind techniques, and integrating mind-body and his own supernatural means. It would be fair to say that there is a definite 'air of mystery' regarding the rituals and ceremonies of old. This is simply due to the fact Magicians created them in the first place. Believing in necessitating the 'long haul' of the apprenticeship. It looked good for them and out of reach for everyone else. The more complex and intriguing the more superior and condescending they appeared to the novice and the rest of the baffled fools. Medieval magick and alchemy have great difficulty in 'crossing over' into the modern world without losing the power of secrecy, mystery, and the unnecessary accoutrements. Today we have so many different forms of inter-communicating, that it is almost laughable to think that it is a requirement to continue to use the 'Old Magickal' formulas. They serve no purpose other than to drive you 'crazy' trying to do them. So perhaps that is the state of mind you needed. Today it is a matter of 'emptying' the mind not 'filling' it.

The old-style ritualistic paraphernalia is not needed to represent that which science explains simplistically. Understanding the true Alchemy, is transformation of the 'self' as 'spirit in matter' trapped and unaware of itself, as a divine and celestial being. Transformation from the 'sleep state of the silent soul,' to the divine and higher self. Now you can comprehend the 'path home' is purely self-realization, of the higher divine you, aware of its natural state. Alchemy of the spirit consciousness is the awakening of the soul, it is the gold as the golden pure Light, manifesting in the material physical dense form.

Magick Begins in The Mind - The mind has a powerful command and control over physical matter, not just your own mind and physical being but that of others too. Magick begins first on the 'inner planes,' causing changes, and then 'something' to happen in the outer world. Cause and effect. Get used to the idea that you have been fooled into believing what you need to do to cause' magick to happen. It is all lies and unnecessary nonsense. You do not need to belong to the Golden Dawn, read all Aleister Crowley's complicated books or be a Free Mason either. You do not need to do LBPR, 'Lesser Banishing Pentagram Ritual'. You can just wave your arms around and speak gibberish, it is the same principle. The world has changed, and certain things are just no longer practical, relevant, or necessary. There is no need to spend hours writing journals by candle light; boiling up bats, toads and other ingredients, to create magickal potions; you don't need to gather herbs and plants at dawn or by the light of full moon, or work out complicated astrological charts in order to get a result. You do not need to spend years researching, discovering mountains of information about the magick of 'old' that simply does not transfer to a modern world. Most people are afraid to 'open up' to communication with the Magickal or Higher self ...why? Because other people have scared them into thinking that it will attract spirits and demons. Why do they say such things? Perhaps they do not want you to discover how powerful you really are. Religion has done it for centuries. Did you know Religion and Magick are ideas in common? The difference being, that Magick empowers you and religion empower the Priest. Demystification simply takes away the power from the magician/priests and gives it back to you. The art of Magick begins with you drawing out your hidden strengths and powers and using them to attract what you want to experience.

Power over 'Free Will' and 'Choice'- The power to choose and cause' things to become realities. For those who understand the meaning of magick and intend to allow the rest of the population to have a little 'peek-in', do so for these reasons. They have power over you, simply by the fact they are not letting you 'join the select club' or 'in on the secret'. They know that in truth there is NO real mystery or secret, and the basic foundation of 'Real Magick' is very simple and hidden in plain view, that you are more likely to be doing magick without knowing or understanding it already. Simply by default. The sacred/secret rituals, will have you pulling your hair out ever before you get to understand just why you are following these 'archaic', 'old hat' and 'past there sell by date' ideas'. I believe that the significance and importance of the ability to shift consciousness is the 'key' to magick, without which it is simply pompousness and posturing. I also believe this 'supernatural' magickal powers manifest from inside a person and not directly from a ritual. Because the ritual is the action of the thoughts and gives expression to what is happening on the inner planes. However, the magickal power is limitless through shifting consciousness and dependent upon the extent of desire, intent and directed 'will'. Therefore, the hidden power is achievable through the 'act' of evoking emotions and consciously attaching them to the desire. This creates the necessary components for the magickal power to be uninhibited, unleashed and set-free to 'work'. Nevertheless, it is believed that magick takes years to achieve and understand. I guess in a way that is true, if you decide to continue to follow those 'olde worlde' ideals, and principles. Yet the basic principles must apply and are always there, in the most obvious and evident way. I learned a great deal about 'Real Magick' at source in Africa. It is raw, unadulterated, natural, and unmodified. Simple and easy and it works without all the nonsense ritual and paraphernalia that 'old magick' requires of you, for the ritual to manifest your desires. Magickal practices only became complicated when man learned the art of writing and added or subtracted and created a system, that was too complicated for most ordinary people to entertain.

Magick Is About State - We engage in habits and routines all the time. You can consider a ritual any routine that is designed for a specific purpose. It is part of how we function. And you might be inclined to say there is nothing magickal in getting ready for a date/interview or any other important meeting. But you would be wrong, to think that you are not creating a 'magickal act,' or a 'ritual,' because you are engaging in 'wishful thinking'. The first caveat for any ritual is- 'be careful what you wish for,' and I would add to that, 'be careful how you are wishing.' Before you do anything, it is the purpose behind any exercise that needs to be clear first. Get your intention organized. Your intention will influence your behaviour, perceptions, and expectations. Predetermining your life simply suggests there is no destiny, or fate, which hinder, or control, the devoted soul. Everything is relative to something. Thoughts create realities. Positive thoughts and deeds create the highest experience.

Negative thoughts and deeds could be called Karma. Everything is Relative.

"When forced to summarize the general theory of relativity in one sentence: time and space and gravitation have no separate existence from matter."
-Albert Einstein

Karma - The word Karma means "deed" or "act" and is related to the concept of action and reaction. This is summed up in the Bible with the phrase 'As you sow, so ye shall reap,' and in the everyday expression, 'What goes around, comes around.' This has been expanded in popular New Age beliefs to relate to the Law of Cause and Effect. Karma is often associated to reincarnation as Karma is also called the wheel of life. It presents the idea that in this life you pay for something you did wrong in a previous life. Reincarnation is associated with some religions but not all. Just so that no one is left out, for those that do not believe in Reincarnation, then there is Instant Karma. However, from a Buddhist perspective Karma is not about punishment and retribution, Karma is all that you are and ever have been. This is framed by your beliefs and expectations about the world and other people. Your worldview is going to determine not only what you attempt but also what you attract to you. From the Magickal perspective that I am presenting, Karma can be thought of because of the principle of 'Like attracts Like.'

Karmic Symbol

The Never-Ending Knot

THE ART OF MAGICKAL STATES

The Art of Magickal States

There is a higher order to the universe, that order can be influenced. Everything you believe to be true, becomes true for you.

What can magick do for you? How can it be applied in business? When will you see results?

Things can change very quickly and ...the keys to...
* Confidence and self-esteem
* Mental and physical balance and power
* Certainty and conviction
* Control emotions
* The law of attraction
* Intensify state of passion
* Magnetism and Charisma
* Relaxation, de-stressing
* Energized, vitality
* Higher levels of awareness
* Change / alter state easily
* See things in a different perspective
* Solve problems
* Change habits and old patterns of belief
* Remote Influence
* Psychic attack and defense

Your Thoughts Create Your Reality
'Inactive' these are Negative Thoughts
* Vague mental images

- Dispersed and scattered thoughts
- Unable to sustain a course of action
- No positive results
- No disciplined thinking
- Moderate
- Lack intensity
- Uneven, fanciful
- Constantly changing direction
- Undeveloped mental concepts
- Hesitation, stop start
- Difficulty with decision-making
- Wavering. Vacillation

'Active' these are Positive Thoughts

- Detailed
- Precise mental images
- Excellent psychic power
- Composed and lucid thoughts that flow constantly
- Powerful thinking patterns
- Decided opinions
- Imposing 'Will' on others
- Unambiguous
- Specific commands
- Authoritative
- Unassailable

What is Magick all about? - Most people will have had some thoughts, ideas and maybe even a little practice of spellbinding, wishful thinking, prayers or trying rituals. Also, some idea about what magick means to them. And that would be my first question to you?

What Does Magick Mean to You? - Magick is there for everyone who wishes to experience it. And as such, I am merely pointing/guiding to creating 'Magickal States' that are necessary for Magick to work, and changes to happen. These changes are the causation of the effects by which you perceive yourself and everything around you to be. Change or alter that perspective and open the mind to 'image' and 'see' differently takes a little time and practice. But you can and will achieve amazing results in just 6 weeks of concentration, attention to detail, and changing old patterns of belief. You may call it 'ritual' or 'routine' an 'exercise' or 'practice' the language is not important the 'idea' and 'action' is.

A Different Approach - Learning the difference between what others perceive or believe magick to be and what magick is. How everything is connected, and nothing is separate. Things that appear to be isolated are in fact belonging to part of something else. Things that seem to be outside of yourself are part of you, as you are part of it. We are all part of creation coming from the one source. We are all connected through this divine energy. This energy consists of the four elements and the spirit of consciousness. How magick operates and functions.

Modern View - For many people, the word Magick calls to mind images of Lord of the Rings and Harry Potter. For other people, the word Magick means medieval sorcerers such as Merlin summoning up storms, archaic rituals, chanting magickal words and using all sorts of paraphernalia. Or witches casting spells by moonlight.

A simple, yet profound way to approach old magick, is to strip away what doesn't work in a modern world and simply use the basic 'principles' and give it a fresh and more up to date look.

7

MAGICK AND MYSTERY

Magick and Mystery

Why does Magick have a 'k'... it is to distinguish between stage Magic, illusion, and tricks. It was Aleister Crowley's notion that Magic is simply sleight of hand, smoke, and mirrors whereas, Universal or Cosmic Magick are the elements, knowledge and change of state that cause things to alter and manifest. Magick, in the context of Aleister Crowley's Thelema, is a term used to show and differentiate the occult from performance Magic and is defined as "the Science and Art of causing Change to occur in conformity with *Will*", including "mundane" acts of will as well as ritual magick.

> - *Aleister Crowley (1875-1947) founded the religion of Thelema. He was largely associated with modern occultism and influenced other religious founders such as Wicca's Gerald Gardner and Scientology's L. Ron Hubbard.*
> - *Aleister Crowley was an English occultist, ceremonial magician, poet, painter, novelist, and mountaineer. He founded the religion of Thelema, identifying himself as the prophet entrusted with guiding humanity into the Æon of Horus in the early 20th century. A prolific writer, he published widely over the course of his life.*

There are too many myths and misconceptions about magick. Understanding how magick works in the modern world, you will need to acquire a fresh perspective and discover information that is more accessible and easily explained. The ancient manuscripts tend to lead you around in circles, by using a language no longer relevant in the 21st century. The old methods are intimidating to a novice, they are meant to be, so that you give up. It would be fair to say that there is a definite 'air of mystery' regarding the rituals and ceremonies. This basically is due to the fact magicians created them in the first place, necessitating the 'long haul' of the apprenticeship? It is the consensus that magick must remain mysteriously out of reach for us, with the exception given only to the dedicated magician and his apprentice. Learning magick is like stepping into a 'labyrinth', you lose your 'lower self' or 'ordinary-self' on the way in and everything you thought was real to you, and discover your 'higher-self' or 'magickal-self' and the way things really are on the way out.

Therefore, in doing so, you do not need the 'lower self' or 'egotist personality' that you believe yourself to be. You do need to awaken and communicate to the 'higher self', so that you can identify with being Magickal. Medieval Magick and alchemy have great difficulty in 'crossing over' into the modern world without losing the power of secrecy, mystery, and paraphernalia.

The art of magick is practiced through an intermediary called 'Ritual', you could easily call it a routine or exercise, if you want to give it a more up to date approach. Magick is a conceptual ethereal system. It emphasizes man's proficiency to assert influence and control the 'natural' world through mind techniques and paranormal mysterious means. Today we have so many different forms of inter-communication that it almost seems laughable, to think that it is a requirement to use the 'Old Magickal' formulas. They serve no purpose other than driving you crazy trying to understand the archaic system. If you are looking for a greater understanding of esoteric knowledge, it can be the journey of a lifetime. There are numerous sources of information that usually result in confusion and bewilderment. However, if you want down-to-earth practical exercises that you can apply to your own life immediately, then here is a source of knowledge that is easily reached and achieved.

Nothing exists without intention.

Imagination is everything, it is the preview of life's coming attractions
- Albert Einstein 1879-1955

What is Magick? - A simple, yet profound way to consider old magick, is to strip away what doesn't work in a modern world and simply use the basic 'principles' and give it a fresh more up to date methodology. Most people will have had some thoughts, ideas and maybe even a little practice of spellbinding, wishful thinking, prayers, chanting or trying rituals. Also, some idea about what magick means to them, and that would be my first question to you?

What Does Magick Mean to You? - Magick is there for everyone who wants to experience it, and as such, I am merely pointing/guiding to how you can start creating 'Magickal States' that are necessary for the work, and changes to transpire. These changes are the effects of causation, by which you perceive yourself and everything around you to be. Change or alter that perspective, open the mind to 'image' and 'see' then perceive differently, takes a little time and practice. But you can, and will achieve amazing results, in just six weeks of concentration, attention to detail, and changing old patterns of belief. Unlike old magick, that requires years to understand and experience to even comprehend the language, symbols and referencing. You may call it 'ritual' or 'routine' an 'exercise' or 'practice' in this instant, the language is not important, the 'idea' and 'action' is.

The Stage Magician - Another version of belief is The Stage Magician such as the late 'Paul Daniels' and David Copperfield, Penn, and Teller.

 Think about the stage magician or conjuror for a moment and the illusions they can create. When we are watching a **'magic'** show, something happens on the stage and we have no idea how. It defies all reasoning of our knowledge and understanding of what is possible in the physical world. So, we call it **'magic'**. However, this **'magic'** is always in the mind of the audience because the stage magician is just applying certain principles, using his knowledge and skill to create an effect that is merely an illusion. What appears to be magic to the audience is just sleight-of-hand, or smoke and mirrors. Some people do not want to know how the trick was done, because it takes away the sense of wonder that accompanies it. I am not looking to take away that sense of awe or wonder. The universe is an awesome and wonder -full place where you can create more magick in your own life. When you understand what part, you play in it and how to achieve certain magickal states.

Old Magick Occult Magicians - Let us look at some occult magicians who influenced magick along the way.

Occult, is to say, or is to mean, "That which is hidden"

During the Middle Ages magic in Europe took on many forms. Instead of being able to identify one type of magician, there were many who practiced several types of magic in these times, including: monks, priests, physicians, surgeons, midwives, folk healers, and diviners. The practice of **'magic'** often consisted of using medicinal herbs for healing purposes. Classical medicine entailed magical elements, they would use charms or potions in hopes of driving out a sickness. -**Wiki**

Henry Agrippa

The Three Books of Occult Philosophy

Henry Cornelius Agrippa von Bettelheim was born on September 14, 1486 in Cologne. He died in 1534 or 1535. In 1509 Agrippa began writing his magnum opus, The Three Books of Occult Philosophy was finally published in 1531.Agrippa's thought unites such diverse topics as planetary ruler-ship, occult virtues, enchantments, types of divination, the scales of numbers and their significance, astrological talismans, the Kabbalistic Names of God and the orders of evil spirits.

Francis Barrett

The Magus

Francis Barrett an English Occultist was the author of "The Magus" published in 1801 a book on the occult and magic. Barrett claimed himself to be a student of metaphysics, chemistry, and natural occult philosophy. He gave lessons in magical arts and meticulously translating ancient texts into English such as the Kabala.

This book dealt with the natural magic of herbs and stones, magnetism, talismans and alchemy. It was not very popular until another magician called Eliphas Levi influenced it.

John Dee

John Dee (Queen Elizabeth 1st Astrologer)

Enochian Magick

The angel magick of John Dee and Edward Kelly became known as Enochian magick when it was incorporated into the rituals of the Golden Dawn system of magick. So why did they use the Enochian language? It was mystical and different. It gave them power. Any words or phrases of an unknown language sound magical and powerful, especially when a priest or magician speaks it. Nobody understands and this can be fascinating and mesmerizing. When the Catholic Church gave the mass in English instead of Latin it lost its power and magical appeal. A slow decline of followers began. The modern approach used by the born-again Christians would be 'speaking in tongues.' You can make up what you like, and nobody can dispute it. Gibberish.

Israel Regardie- "They are couched in Biblical language. After all Dee was a Christian in the Elizabethan era and a student of the Bible, so when these calls were received, they had a very Biblical flavor. They may not mean very much, but they sound very impressive and therefore have some emotional value as a stimulus to awaken the magickal power in invocation."

Aleister Crowley

Magick

It was in the early 1900's that the word magic began appearing with a 'k' rather than just the 'c' at the end. This was due to Aleister Crowley the great Magician and author of many books on magick. He intended to separate the real magick with the 'k' from the illusionists and stage performers, pulling rabbits out the hat and juggling balls in the air. As far as Aleister Crowley was concerned they were mere fancy entertainers and tricksters. He described magick as-

'the science and art of causing change to occur in conformity with the will '
Israel Regardie was a student of Crowley's for many years.

Old Thought Magick
There are too many myths and misconceptions about magick.

- The old methods are intimidating to the novice, they are meant to be so that you give up.
- Complicated difficult to read books that drive you crazy.
- Bizarre rituals for no apparent reason
- You do not need to have an altar and all the paraphernalia.
- You do not need to do LBPR or the 'Lesser Banishing Pentagram Ritual'.
- You do not need to gather herbs and plants at dawn.
- You will not attract evil spirits or demons with GOOD intent.
- You do not need to waste time learning sigils.
- You do not have to spend years researching,
- Ancient manuscripts lead you around in circles.
- You do not need to belong to the Golden Dawn.
- Read all Aleister Crowley's complicated books or be a Free Mason.
- The 'long haul' of the apprenticeship is old hat.
- 'Old Magickal' formulas. They serve no purpose other than driving you crazy trying to understand the archaic system.
- Ancient writings do not equate in the modern world.
- Kabbalah and its ancient Jewish mysteries.

Too Much Confusion - Because you are most likely to be already confused about magick, here are some insights.

- There is no magick in the specific words used in rituals. Magick is in the resonance and vibration. It is not a perquisite to learn a magickal language that someone else 'made up' for his or her rituals and purposes. You can use any gibberish to clear your mind of old clutter, call to the higher realms or sound magickal. However, using some specific 'words' in a particular 'tone' creates a meaningful vibration, causing alignment with the higher realms.

- You do not need to have an altar and all the paraphernalia. The paraphernalia such as a plate, knife, chalice, and candle are outward physical representations of the elements that you are made up of, as earth, air, water, and fire. The mind imaging and visualizing is the true altar, not placing symbolic objects on a table. To 'see' in your mind you need to have experiences of the natural elements and how they affect you emotionally.

- It is unnecessary to read hundreds of old magick books, [I have]. Trying to cross-reference and understand the correspondences, that have no use in a modern world is far too time consuming. The books tend to lead you into a 'maze'. Ancient writings do not equate in the modern world. That is merely pre-experimentalism. The art of magick is finding the right way in and out of higher consciousness, and not filling that space with unnecessary jargon, that serves no useful purpose.

- You do not need to do **LBPR** or the 'Lesser Banishing Pentagram Ritual'. The action of the arms moving and pointing in different directions is simply an outward expression as you consciously connect to the four corners of the universe, or north, south, east, and west. The physical movements of waving your arms around will 'mix' up your aura, aligning your energy field to the universe.

- You do not need to gather herbs and plants at dawn. Except if you enjoy getting up early to observe the sun rising and the day breaking. Or you are an herbalist. Or you want to observe the elements. By observing the natural rhythms of nature and understanding the way it operates, you will soon become aware of your part in it.

- You will not attract evil spirits or demons with **GOOD** intent. If your intentions are positive in nature, for the highest good of all, you cannot attract negativity. You only receive what you transmit. You cannot attract negative thoughts and feeling when in a higher state of consciousness.

- You do not need to waste time learning sigils. Simply write something in an ancient language i.e. Sanskrit, Japanese, Arabic, Aramaic, or Hebrew it is not easily recognizable to the mind. You then attach a specific meaningful concept to the 'pictogram or kanji' so that you have a focal point of reference. It is a symbol for the sub-conscious mind only.

- You do not need to belong to the Golden Dawn, read all Aleister Crowley's complicated books or be a Free Mason either. The old-style ritualistic paraphernalia is no longer needed to represent that which science explains simplistically. The world has changed, and certain things are just no longer practical, relevant, or necessary.

- You do not have to spend years researching, discovering mountains of information about the magick of old that simply does not transfer to a modern world. The sacred/secret rituals will have you pulling your hair out ever before you get to understand just why you are following these 'archaic', 'old hat' and 'past there sell by date' ideas.

No Real Mystery - The more time you spend discovering what you do not need, the less time you must practice and do it. It is said that magick takes many years to perfect and understand. I guess in a way that is true, if you wish to continue following the old ideas, and philosophy. Learning the art of becoming magickal does not necessarily need to be incomprehensible, perplexing or time consuming. There's NO real mystery to Magick, it is so simple and hidden in plain sight like so many secrets, that you are likely to be doing magick without knowing or understanding it already, simply by default. Therefore, I believe it is fair to say that magick is predetermining what you want to experience in your life. This basically means no fate or accident, to obstruct or control the committed souls journey home. The supernatural, the unexplained, and the mysterious, unsolved...Magick, in the broadest sense, is any act designed to cause intentional change, a conscious direction of will accomplish a goal. However, the basic principles must apply and are always there, in the most obvious and evident way.

I believe that the significance and importance of the ability to shift consciousness, is the 'key' to any magickal intent, without which, it is purely pretentiousness and pomposity. I also believe the 'supernatural' powers required, manifest inside us and not directly from a formal procedure. Because the 'action of the thoughts' gives expression to what's happening on the inner planes. Through the act of 'changing state', evoking one's emotions and attaching them to a desired intention, changes are accomplished. This course of action creates the necessary components for the process of magickal powers to be uninhibited. The Genii.

Within us there is an innate power that is limitless, dependent upon the extent of desire, intent and directed 'will'. It is achievable through the 'act' of evoking emotions and consciously attaching them to the desire. It is believed that real magick takes years to perfect and I guess in a way that is true, if you continue to follow the 'olde worlde' ideas, you will be practicing forevermore. Yet, the basic principles must apply in a modern world, and are always there in the most obvious and evident way. It is not about adding stuff to your life; it is about tapping into the inherent nature of the universe. You do not need abundance in your life, the universe is naturally abundant, if you can only listen to it and connect with it and allow it.

> "Begin doing what you want to do now. We are not living in eternity. We have only this moment, sparkling like a star in our hand-and melting like a snowflake..."
> **-Marie Beyon Ray**

8

CHANGING STATE OR MAGICK

Changing State or Magick

- The art of bringing about changes in the physical world by use of the power of the mind; action in accordance with will.
- A natural practice of mind over matter.
- The art of focusing your will and emotions to effect change in the world around you and the world within you.
- The act of focusing the energies of the Universe to effect needed change on the mundane plane.
- The use of natural energies within ourselves, and the world around us to effect a physical change in a condition or life situation.
- Something that you visualize in your mind and bringing it into being in the physical world. This is done by force of will.
- An interconnection in the cosmos that connects and binds all things above and beyond the natural forces.
- Through the act of 'changing state', evoking one's emotions and attaching them to the intention, changes are accomplished. This course of action creates the necessary components for the process of magickal powers to be uninhibited.
- To create the right state, to cause intentional change, conscious direction of will and accomplish your goals you need to believe in yourself, and your potentiality.
- Man's proficiency to assert influence and control the 'natural' world through mind techniques and paranormal means.

What Stops Magick? - If you do not follow the strategy step by step with the power of certainty and conviction you will end up in a cul-de-sac and going nowhere, or at least back where you started.

1. Not listening to intuition.
2. Not believing in yourself.
3. Not opening and closing exercise ritual properly.
4. Unbalanced.
5. No direction.
6. Missing something out of a ritual/exercise.
7. Missing out details in imaging.
8. Not forgiving.
9. Attaching the wrong emotion.
10. Not de-cluttering your mind and filling with good stuff.

- Not listening to intuition. Ignoring the 'gut feeling' and going ahead regardless. Or when you know it just does not feel good, or right but you continue anyway. Difficulty with decision-making 'is it intuition or my own mind'?
- Not believing in yourself. Kidding yourself instead of absolute certainty and confidence beyond doubt. Hesitation stop start. You need to be authoritative.
- No direction. Unclear messages of desire and intention. Unable to sustain a course of action. Constantly changing direction. Lack intensity. Unclear ideas and thoughts.
- Missing something out of the strategy. Loosing focus during the process does not work. It must be well planned, practiced and rehearsed with dedicated commitment.
- Missing out details in imaging. Not 'seeing' what you want clearly in your mind's eye. Vague mental images and dispersed and scattered thoughts. No disciplined thinking. You must have precise mental images.
- Not forgiving. If you are unable to forgive your own poor choices and others theirs, you will continue to hold negative patterns that attract more of the same. The simple act of forgiving clears old unwanted emotions, that get in the way of being in control and feeling good about yourself.
- Attaching the wrong emotion. You must be very precise when attaching an

emotion. Some emotions are obvious like fire/passion. Be certain of what it is you are trying to attract in your life, or what will be attracted to you and what the higher purpose for it is?

- Not de-cluttering your mind and filling it with good stuff detailed congruent messages. You need to have composed and lucid thoughts, that flow constantly with powerful thinking patterns and clear decided opinions. Good positive thoughts and feelings.

What is Ritual? Routine, Exercise or Ritual?

- A Ritual is a primary focusing mechanism that allows consequential innate powers to be directed at *will*, to the fulfilment of desired intent.

Or it could be-

- A ceremony consisting of elaborate and ornate paraphernalia required by the practitioner is a Ceremonial-Ritual. Magickal and Religious Rituals both fit into this category.

Since ancient times rituals have been performed as an important part of all sacred and magickal ceremonies, bringing about desired and specific objectives. A ritual consists of an exact configuration set out by mental preparation, focused intent, including mental, verbal, and physical actions. It is through these actions that the power of magick is then unhindered and released. A ritual is a way of accessing the powerful abundant and copious 'physic forces', that differentiates itself outside of 'normal awareness' and is subject to deliberate communication. Rituals are preformed subconsciously every day, however small they may appear to be, like saying 'hello', shaking hands and blowing a kiss. But when 'directed *will*' is absent to create desired changes, these simple rituals are a mere habitual version of the original concept. One of the most common rituals preformed today is that of blowing out candles on a birthday cake and making a wish. This ritual has desired intent. 'I wish', therefore more potent because there is thought and feeling, but it lacks the magickal ingredient of 'directed *will*'.

We engage in rituals all the time. It is part of who we are. The reptilian part of our brain is devoted to ritualization and habitualism. The most essential feature of any ritual is symbolism and actions, that are deliberately chosen yet not dictated by any logic or reasoning. I believe that the significance and importance of the ability to shift consciousness is the key to any ritual, without which it is simply pretentiousness and audacious bravado.

Magick is ever-present, it is ubiquitous and prevalent, but it is necessitated and preformed through the vehicle of the ritual. I believe the supernatural magickal powers, manifest from inside the person and not directly from the ritual. However, the magickal power is limitless through the manipulation of consciousness, dependent upon the magnitude of desire and intent, in addition to inspiring life into the symbolism. Through the act of evoking one's emotions and attaching them to the symbols, it inevitably creates the necessary components for the process of magickal powers to be without hindrance.

[symbols and symbolism in this case simply means those images you create in your mind]

What are these natural innate powers hidden inside us? The entire universe. Once you have practiced for a while, you can create a strong enough sense of certainty without having to go through a full ritual. You are simply setting up by habit, a time to release thoughts and feelings desired for the intent. Magick is not that difficult. It is just a matter of knowing what to practice. The first thing you ought to know is that you will not require a collection of paraphernalia to be magickal. They look great and serve a purpose to focus on, but they simply represent the elements regardless of ornamental value. For these exercises you will need frankincense pure essential oil, incense, some candles and a cushion or mat plus the desire to explore and discover.

Magick can help you become more charismatic and attract the things you desire. You will also be able to have more control over your own state and can tap into confidence and energy when you need it. This does take well-directed practice, to get results. However, once you have put in the energy and focus there will come a time when you will just go into your magick automatically. If you do not try to practice, then you can easily say, it didn't work. However, with a little well focussed exercise, you can start getting results. Attitude is everything: focussed intention, followed by gratitude. To be able to manifest wonderful things in your life, you must have the right attitude, and then be grateful for the gift. Nine times out of ten, people have the wrong state attached to what they are trying to achieve.

To know that you are the creator of your own reality, allows you to expand beyond the limited mind and belief system, that you have been taught. Since you cannot know what is, or what is not possible, it makes sense to believe in more possibilities than less. Believing that endless possibilities are available to you, is the first step. Then allow your thoughts to dip into other dimensions and realities beyond the physical every day, to experience the spirit or invisible world and all its amazing gifts. By practising these magickal exercises, you will learn how to balance your mental and emotional bodies, energise yourself with breathing, and remove stale energy and old thought forms out of your body and more. We are creatures of habit by nature. There are things you do every day, that you do your way because that is what you are used to. There exists routine in everyone's life, even if that is just the natural rhythm of the day, or your body. When we formalise certain habits and routines and perform them with a specific purpose in mind, we can refer to them as rituals. Just think about when you get ready to go out, on a date, or for an interview. You have intention and purpose to getting ready, dressing up and moving forward. That is the kind of experience you are going to create, except you'll be more specific about the intention and more directed in the preparation and routine. There is a way to incorporate magickal exercises into everyday activities and later I'm also going to give you suggestions for how you can do what you are going to do anyway and use that as an opportunity for practice. We can even turn the mundane everyday tasks into something more useful and even exciting, but first let us focus on your ritual.

Importance of Preparation - Before attempting to do any kind of ritual, you need to know why you are doing this. There needs to be a clear reason for the exercise and practice. It may be to create a state of confidence and certainty, manifest a relationship, or just be open to whatever information you might receive.

Create a Sacred Space - When you perform a ritual or routine, you need to do something that marks this out as separate from your everyday life and normal activities. You will need some physical space in which to do the exercise and you could use a rug, to mark out a sacred space. You will also need to prepare yourself to enter that space, but first let me describe some of the ways you can step away from your everyday world and begin to create some magick for yourself. As with anything once you practice, you may find that you do not need to go through every step-in order to achieve the right state. Practise becomes the norm after a short period of doing it.

Sacred or Magickal Space implies an area where you go to create special thoughts or to unwind and meditate. You can clear your thoughts more easily in a calming environment, purposefully arranged for higher and magickal consciousness to function in.

Mental Space - As well as physical space, you will also need some mental space. When you are preparing for your magickal exercises, you must first de-program the clutter and negative thoughts from your mind and begin to think positively and powerfully, to have any effect on change. The first thing to do is to take a few deep breaths through your nostrils, and exhale through your mouth. Do this three times and notice the difference in how you feel. When you become practiced at reaching a quiet state of mind, it may only require that you say to yourself something like- 'I clear my mind of all chatter and all negative thoughts, that might hinder the process of creating my sacred space.' Until you can do that, or if your mind is busy you might require some extra help, especially if you have had a stressful day. You will need to empty your mind of all the chatter and clutter that creates the inner dialogue. There is a constant flow of information coming into our minds even with eyes closed, it creeps in and disturbs the harmony that you wish to experience. A quick way to stop the internal chatter, is to stick your tongue out and hold it. The tongue is connected to the part of the brain that produces your internal dialogue. Try that now and you will notice that it goes quiet in your mind.

A more elegant method that you can use in public, is where you place the tip of your tongue on the roof of your mouth just behind your front teeth. I use various techniques to clear my mind of all the everyday stuff that gets in the way, such as old unwanted patterns, hang-ups, and cluttered memories, that I no longer need. Think of it as having a mental spring clean.

For example, imagine writing it all on a blackboard in your mind, and really fill it with all the things that have been taking your attention. Once you have filled it up and feel that everything is on the blackboard, take a breath and then wipe it clean, so that you have a clear head. You can also imagine it on a misty window, then shatter the glass. Sometimes I pretend that I have forgotten to switch on the monitor for my internal computer. Which means even though the computer is on, I cannot access any of the information. It's just a blank screen. If you are not good at imagining the blackboard, window or computer, you can actually write everything onto a piece of paper and then screw it all up, and throw it away or even set fire to it. Remember, the intention it to get unwanted thoughts out of your head, so whatever you do to achieve it, then that is good. Use your own imagination. If a feeling really persists you can shake yourself out of it. It is something we do naturally when we shudder. The quick physical movement of shaking out a feeling from your body is enormously powerful. You can also turn around a few times, clap your hands and slap your thighs, clank some saucepans to make some noise. Do this loud enough to create the startle reflex and it will change how you feel very quickly. Feelings tend to hang around because of the chemicals floating through your system, and they sometimes need a bit of encouragement to move them on.

The Structure of a Ritual - The first caveat for any ritual, practises, or exercise, is 'be careful what you wish for'. You can create your own practices once you understand the principals involved. I will be giving many examples throughout the book, but they are all based on the same principle. For a ritual to be effective here is what I believe you need to do. You may find your own variations on these ideas, but here is what I believe needs to be there.

- Intention first

- Preparation

- Create a sacred space

- Clearing you mind or Deprogram

- Your statement of your intent

- Reprogram

- Energize yourself

- Offering

- Completion

- Let go

As with anything, once you practice you may find that you do not need to go through every single step to achieve the right state. Practise becomes the norm after a short period of doing it.

Intention First - Before attempting to do any kind of ritual you need to know why you are doing this. There needs to be a clear reason for the exercise and practice. The first caveat for any ritual is 'be careful what you wish for,' and I would add to that, 'be careful how you are wishing.' Before you do anything, it is the purpose behind any exercise that needs to be clear first. Get your intention accurate. Your intention will influence your behaviour, perceptions, and expectations. As you progress, you can define your own intentions and here are a few guidelines about how to define your intention. Be sure you know exactly what you want to attract into your life. Remember all the stories and fairy tales about the person who gets three wishes, and gets exactly what they wish for, except they were not clear enough. Be truly clear with precise details. If you want love you must say what kind of love, motherly, sisterly, or romance? It could be finance so you must state if it is money owed to you, a credit card, or your debts cleared?

Although we start from simply asking, what do we want? The state you come from is not one of 'wanting.' Pleading and begging are a weakness of man and supplication is not going to get you what you yearn for. It is in your awareness of your strength and true power, that the prayer is answered. Prayer means to command and expectation, not to grovel to your maker. When we plead forgiveness, we expose our feebleness to the universe, it is going to ignore you. Why? The universe is great and powerful not small and weak. If you are calling out to God for help, then forget it God will expect you to help yourself. Why? Your creator gave you the power, use it. Connecting to your Divine, Higher or Magickal You are all one and the same thing. History tells us that these types of names, have always existed about that part of us that is the 'unseen' or 'spirit being'. In the first place we are all higher beings or spirit essence having a physical experience on the material plane.

Here are examples of intentions-

- Deliberately connecting to your Magickal You.

- Relaxation, Inner Peace or Meditation

- Seeking help for a problem, health or emotional.

- Send and receive healing, loving and compassionate thoughts.

- Protection for someone, psychic attack, or defence.

- Giving or Receiving Goods, Financial or other.

- Confidence, Self Esteem, Power and Control

- Receive guidance

These examples are so you may understand how to create a state of confidence and certainty, manifest a relationship, or just be open to whatever information you might receive. When you are clear on what your intention is and you have formulated it clearly, then it's time to prepare for the ritual. How to achieve communicating with the Cosmic or Universal Mind, you need to fully understand the Four Elements in Nature that are inside and outside of us. Once you understand how they function and operate it becomes easy to utilize them in thoughts and deeds to get where you want to be. There are different ways to approach their meaning and reality, here I give you a few examples of the types of ideas to have a better insight to what they can be known as. There are many books available with different views on the subject matter, some more basic and fundamental, and others with a deeper esoteric meaning.

Examples - The way I use the four elements to prepare a room for magickal practice or teaching is different. I use candles and incense to dry out the moisture in the room, so I am removing any information that is already there, in the atmosphere. I create Holy Water blessed with my intention. I flick it around or drink a little, to mouth spray into the air. I also swallow some. When you practice, you need to create a sense that you are doing something that is outside of your everyday life. You want to eliminate any existing associations and make the rituals something that is distinctly different, from what you normally do.

Examples - You could use a special rug, mat or a colorful throw or sheet to 'mark' that out as a sacred space. Create a physical circle using candles, not the tall ones they are easily knocked over. Please use candles wisely, do not forget you are working with the FIRE element here, put them in a dish and better still, use the ones that float in water. Now you have two active elements. Small stones or crystals (another element as earth) or colorful ribbon looks amazing when they are interwoven together. Get seven ribbons one for each chakra/zone. Silk scarves. Colored discs can be affective too, hand painted by you, on wood or colored cardboard, and again, it is more interesting to be creative, so the seven colors of the spectrum are a perfect expression. You may like to use dried flower heads or the wooden ones. Marbles, or even wooden curtain rings. Do not use plastic, rubber, or synthetic material please. As you become better or more practiced you can create an imaginary circle. You will also need to prepare yourself to enter that space, but first let me describe some of the ways you can step away from your everyday world and begin to create some magick for yourself.

Preparing the Room - The prepared sacred space/room is filled with smoke from the incense, and I only ever use Nag Champa, (Sai Baba blue packet and hologram sealed) or the best frankincense sticks or resin on charcoal. This is the process of smudging your aura to eliminate negative energies around you, and in the room. The candles or night-lights are safe and secure and burning. Ring a bell or crystal glass to clear the 'stuck energy sounds' it's now clear of old negative thought forms and vibrations. I create an imaginary bubble/mini atmosphere and blow into it filling up the entire room and step inside it. It is like blowing up a balloon and stepping into it. I see the colors of the spectrum and know that I am perfectly safe to begin. I make sure it is sealed. I do this by pretending to lock it with my imaginary key or zipping it up. Now I am totally protected (contained in a sacred circle or bubble) I am opening the portal. When you are bathing blow bubbles and get familiar with the idea of what you are undertaking, and a sense of what you are doing it for.

Structure of a Ritual - We engage in habits and routines all the time. You can consider a ritual any routine that is designed for a specific purpose. It is part of how we function. Before attempting to do any kind of ritual you need to know why you are doing it. There needs to be a clear reason for the exercise and practice. That may be to create a state of confidence and certainty, manifest a relationship or just be open to whatever information you might receive. Ritual requires you to fully understand the meanings of visual, verbal, and physical and how the ritual fits together.

9

THE 7 MINUTE RITUAL

The 7 Minute Ritual - Remember to attach the correct Element/or Elements to your ritual/routine. It is always about the state you are in that determines the outcome.

1. Desired Intent
2. Clear Your Mind
3. Pick a Direction or Goal
4. Create a Representation
5. Add Feelings
6. Projection Through Mind and Breath
7. Take Physical Action

Exercise Breathing Techniques - Here are 3 simply 'change of state' breathing techniques.

1. **Four-Fold**: Inhale through your nose to the count of 4, hold for 4 and exhale through your mouth, to 4 make a sound like Haaah.

2. **Sanchin:** The tip of your tongue pressed up to the roof of your mouth and breathe in through your nose for 3 seconds and out through your mouth for 7 seconds. As you inhale only push your stomach out like a balloon not your chest. As you exhale pull your stomach in and tighten your muscles and imagine gathering energy at the hara point (2 inches below the naval)

3. **Fire/Dragon:** inhale and exhale rapidly through the nose 7 times, pause and take a long inhale and exhale to prevent hyperventilation.

Energy Balance Routine - Intention and desire, clear and precise picture, or vision of what it is you are attracting to yourself. Have bare feet or socks only. Open the Ritual by creating a sacred space to work in, create the circle, or a bubble of energy to feel safe in. You are going to Open Up your energy field through your Aura and Chakras.

Create the Sacred Space - Take a deep breath and slowly blow out, as if you are blowing and creating a bubble from your breath. Picture those soapy bubbles and see it growing bigger and bigger, then fill the entire room. Now physically step inside it and seal it up, with a swift action. Open your own energy field, with the first 2 fingers of right hand, touching just below the lower lip. Making a swift action, going downwards and out at the pubic bone area, as if you are sweeping through all the energy zones-chakras, then flicking the energy away at the base zone your pubic area.

15 seconds.

NEXT STEP

Now make a fist with your right hand, and make 3 thumps on your thymus like Tarzan, it is the hard bone in the center of the chest.

Now locate the 2 points just below your collarbone, just below the 2 knobby bones and feel for the soft pockets. Now with both hands tap hard, on these areas for about 5 seconds. It should feel uncomfortable. Now press your fingers all around your ribs, just below the breast line, it should feel sore. But tap and push your thumbs in, for 5 seconds.

15 seconds.

NEXT STEP

Now sit upright on a hard chair and place your left leg over your right knee and left palm of hand holding bottom of foot with right hand crossing over and holding top of foot. Breathe deeply through your nose and out through mouth.

Sit for 5 seconds and then change to right leg resting on left knee and right-hand holding bottom of foot with left hand crossing and holding top of foot sit for 5 seconds breathe deeply through your nose and out from your mouth to the sound of Haaaa

10 seconds.

NEXT STEP

Mind Juggling.

With feet flat to ground, legs slightly apart, put your left hand over right hand and hold pressure points on forehead, between the hairline and eyebrows, then press firmly for 10 seconds. Scramble your Thoughts and say aloud, any nonsense gibberish. Back to front words made up words, or something that you think is Magick-al. Then 'close your eyes' and take a deep breath through your nose, and out of mouth to the sound of Haaa, as you drop your hands and rest them on your lap.

10 seconds.
NEXT STEP

Now with both hands, begin to pull and stretch your forehead, so begin with fingers touching in the center of forehead and pull gently, as they separate. Do this 3 times. Now rub your head with your fingers and back of your neck, then ruffle your hair. Pull your hair gently and then stretch and pull on your scalp, you will feel the scalp moving. Now press fingers into the pockets just below your cheekbones, take a deep breath and exhale, repeat 3 times. Now with your right hand, press your fingers on the back of your left hand, just behind the knuckles and in-between your ring finger and your little finger. Hold the pressure there, then tap for about 20 seconds breathing and inhaling through your nose, exhaling through your mouth. And open your eyes.

1 minute.

NEXT STEP

Stand Up. Rub your hands together briskly, then clap, jump up and down for 5 seconds.

Now stand with feet apart and stretch both arms in the air, above your head and wave them around from side to side, above you and crossing them over in front of you. Mixing up your energy field. Now stretch one arm up with palm facing up, and the other arm stretching down with the palm facing down. Take a deep breath through your nose and exhale through your mouth and change arms and repeat this 3 times.

Now march on the spot, swinging your arms from side to side opposite to your knees as you raise them up as high as you can. Left knee up and right hand out, right knee up and left hand out.

20 seconds.

NEXT STEP

Mirror and Reflection. Now stand in front of a mirror and observe yourself.

Balance your body weight, stand with feet apart and feel a connection between you and the earth. Do this by imagining a red line of energy going down from your hara, (2 inches below your naval) entering the earth and anchoring it. Be connected to your world, before you enter higher states. Imagine your feet are growing roots and going down deep into the ground. Feel grounded, fixed, and secure, where you are standing. Feel solid, stable, and powerful. Touch and pat your body, feel the shape and size. Balance mind and body feel stuck to the ground.

Place your right hand over your hara, cover it with your left hand.

This takes a minute to achieve... breathing deeply...then...

1 minute

NEXT STEP

Breathing. Start to inhale very deeply through the nose, and out through the mouth and exhale. Move your left hand up over your heart, keep your right hand over your hara and now begin to breathe in 1,2,3,4, and hold for 4 seconds out 1,2,3,4. Get a rhythm going and as you do this tap into your emotions, passion/anger, compassion/love, whatever the feelings are, that you require for the ritual. Begin to feel the emotion and start to expand it, double it. See it getting bigger and moving out into your energy field (aura). Now imagine the emotional energy as a misty white line, moving out of the top of your head and moving down in front of you, then looping through your solar plexus. What is happening is the emotional content has been energized and doubled, expanded by your breathing and you are consciously seeing it moving up through your body. It is now moving out of your crown and circling back into you, through the solar plexus. Each time this energy passes your heart, it becomes more and more powerful. Do this for 2 minutes.

2 minutes.

NEXT STEP
Action. Place both hands over the hara and create a triangle with your fingertips, and your thumbs touching. Now looking in the mirror, project from your mind's eye (3rd eye) a laser beam of energy. Project the image of what you want onto the mirror. As you do this, SEE the image, and hold it there as your intention and desire. Get excited, attach the right feeling to the intent. Stay there for 1 minute. Breathe in through your nose and blow onto the mirror the image your created in your mind.

1 minute.

NEXT STEP
Linking Up
Now with your right middle finger press the image onto your forehead and hold it there for 10 seconds and breath in and out. Keep your finger on your forehead and place the middle finger of your left hand into your naval then press and lift, hold it there for 30 seconds. Now close-up, by sweeping your right hand from the pubic bone, up through the zones and touch the bottom lip, as you do this breathe in through your nose and exhale to the sound of Haaa.

40 seconds.

NEXT STEP
Close the Ritual. Close the act. Now clap your hands turn around a few times, jump up and down, wave your arms all around you and shout Yes, Yes, Yes. And pat yourself on the back and say "it is done...so be it"

10 seconds.
Drink a glass of water, open a window for fresh air and return to normal life, forget about the ritual.

7 STEPS TO GOAL SETTING

7 Steps to Goal Setting

Discover how to turn your goals into realities.

Here are the RITUAL-Routine-Exercises.

Magick is all about causing intentional change, a conscious direction of will accomplish a goal, the basic principles of Magick apply in a modern world and are always there for us to use. I believe that the ability to shift consciousness is the key to any magickal intent. I also believe that 'supernatural' powers manifest from inside a person because the action of the thoughts gives expression to what is happening on the inner planes. This power is limitless when shifting consciousness, but is dependent on the extent of your desire, intent and directed *will*.

How can it help you achieve your goals? - It is not about adding stuff to your life; it is about tapping into the inherent nature of the universe. You do not need abundance in your life, the universe is naturally abundant, if you can only listen to it and connect with it and allow it. Everything you believe to be true becomes true for you. So, to create the right state to cause intentional change, conscious direction of will and accomplish your goals you need to believe in yourself, and your potentiality. It is important to start by being positively clear about what you want to wish for. Make sure that you are heading in the right direction first and follow the strategy step by step, with the power of certainty and conviction. Do not rush, take your time and you will achieve amazing results.

Focus on The Four Elements to assist in the Ritual, Routine- There is extensive information on this in PART TWO.

Fire Energy - Energize in a very intense and expressive way through anger or passion. You can experience this intensity and how to tap into it, in an instant. Mental intelligence and alertness. What happens when you experience this energy?

- Fire up in an instant.
- Create an intense state of passion.
- Project a fire-like energy.
- Feel confident.
- Become magnetic.

Principle- PASSIONATE and POWERFUL

Air Energy - Air Energy is essentially the air that we breathe. It is also known as 'prana' or 'mana' and creates the ki or chi energy, in the body. It is the essence of life. However, learning to breathe differently and more effectively can have a profound impact on more than just your well-being.

- It is the vital force, or key to life
- The means to relaxation and energy.
- What determines your vitality.
- One of the keys to healing and magick.
- Primary, connection with higher self and creator.

Principle COMMUNICATION and VITAL FORCE

Water Energy - Energy that relates to our emotions, it is moving out from the body via water. There is one universal emotion and energy that we call love. Not the head-over-heels romantic notion, but a feeling of complete bliss and unity with the universe. This is the foundation of compassion, forgiveness and how we can see a connection between us all.

- Your emotional brain and chemistry of feelings.
- What determines your behavior.
- One of the keys of the law of attraction.
- Empathy, Sympathy and Compassion

Principle- SENSATIONS and CONNECTEDNESS.

Earth Energy - Energy. You must feel grounded and connected to the earth. When you experience this energy, you are stable and balanced in a physical way, and that allows you to be balanced in other ways too. Good balance is the key to confidence and standing your ground, it also enables you to conjure up vast amounts of good feelings, when you need physical awareness and gravity. Balance and strength will increase your ability to tap into the energy fields.

- A key to confidence and self-esteem.
- A physical reference for mental balance.
- Part of certainty and conviction.
- Physical power, strength, and stability.

Principle- GROUNDED AND FEARLESS.

7 Steps to Goal Setting

First Meditate on what you want to achieve-

1. Fix your desired intent.
2. Clear your mind.
3. Pick a direction or goal.
4. Create an image.
5. Add feelings.
6. Project through your mind and breath.
7. Take physical action.

Step 1: Fix your desired intent

First, you must be positive about what you want. Nothing happens in the universe without intent, so you need to have your intentional desire in place from the start. There must be genuine deep emotions and feelings attached to the desire, so try to form a clear picture in your mind of what it looks, feels, or even smells like. Once you have that vision fixed in your mind, then the next steps become easier, more powerful, and more effective. Remember that your intention is receiving, so whatever you transmit, you get back.

What you Do want is:

- Positive thoughts.
- Detailed mental images.
- Composed and lucid thoughts that flow constantly.
- Powerful thinking patterns.
- Decided opinions.
- Clarity.
- Specific commands.
- Authority.

What you DON'T want is:

- Negative thoughts.
- Vague mental images.
- Dispersed and scattered thoughts.
- Inability to sustain a course of action.
- Undisciplined thinking.
- Moderation and lack of intensity.
- Constantly changing direction.
- Hesitation and wavering.
- Difficulty with decision-making.

Step 2: Clear your mind

Now that you have positive intention, you can move on to freeing up a space in your mind to fill with what you want to experience. You need to remove any obstacles and create a clear space before you can set a new direction for your thinking. It is important that you have clear and positive statements concerning the way you programmed your mind, to believe the desires are certain of arriving. Problem is, many of us spend too much time and energy reinforcing old ideas we have about ourselves. We get so stuck in these old patterns of thinking, that the patterns become 'demons' in our minds. Often, we say we are going around in circles and getting nowhere, but in fact we are going somewhere and that is back to where we started. Then we go off in the same direction again. Sitting and trying to clear your mind, or solve problems rarely works because you are maintaining the body language or physical position, that holds the 'stuck' situation in place.

How to declutter:

Think of a problem you have right now. Notice how your physical posture shifts. Try closing your eyes and take a deep breath. Release it through your mouth, making the sound 'Ah' as you do it. Then stand up, take another deep breath and pace 3 steps forward. Stand still for 3 seconds, holding the breath as you pace 3 steps back, then release the breath. As you breathe in again, imagine white mist being drawn in the breath and as you hold it see your clutter and muddled thoughts enter the mist. Then simply blow them out into the air to disperse them. By doing this simple exercise you allow your mind and body to move to a different time and space and take on a different pattern of thought, from the stuck position. Now it is easier to let go and allow clear and more coherent thoughts to flow. Now you are thinking clearly.

Other things to try:

- Another great example is to hop, skip and jump outside for a few moments. You are breathing in fresh air to energize you and concentrating on another task, so your attention is no longer on the problem.
- Go out and walk up the road until you feel lighter and clearer, then turn around and walk back. (Do not go 'around' the block as you are simply going around in a bigger circle.) When you return to the room, do not sit in the same chair.
- Sing and dance, jump up and down. Sing or make up gibberish in the bath or shower.
- You can really start the process of internal change by having a sense of forgiveness for yourself and others. This creates the right mood and opens your mind to 'see' what you do not need in your life. Think about those moments when you refused to forgive someone, then to let them go simply blow them out of your system, and watch the suppressed feelings, disperse back into the atmosphere.

Step 3: Pick a direction or goal

Now that you have cleared your mind of clutter it is much easier to think about what you want to achieve or to attract. This step is all about setting the direction you want to go in – it might be a career move, a new romance, adventure, wealth, or something else that is relevant for you. The goal you choose for the first time should be reasonably do-able. Do not choose something that is too far out of reach and too far away from your reality just now. Your aim should be something believable and achievable, with some clear thinking and effort put into action. Most people will have some ideas and maybe a little practice of wishful thinking or goal setting and how to achieve it. Magickal goal setting requires you to look closely at what you perceive yourself and everything around you to be. Changing that perspective and opening your mind to see differently takes a little time and practice. But you can and will achieve amazing results in a noticeably short space of time with concentration, attention to detail and by changing your old patterns and beliefs. When you are changing and you're in resonance with that which you want to attract, or to become, then things around you will change too.

Step 4: Create an image

Now that you have a goal to head for it should be easy to image-up a scene in your mind's eye. You need to create a detailed picture in your mind that gives an authentic representation of the goal you wish to achieve. It is this representation that allows you to create the energy and send the signal out to The Universe.

How to visualize:

Think carefully about what you want to manifest and when you can clearly visualize it in your mind, then you can begin the process of building the energy. (If you have not actually had the experience to bring into your mind, you might want to get some help by looking on the Internet or at the TV, DVDs, or books.)

Next, simply imagine yourself running a movie inside your head, of the scene you wish to experience, with you as the star performer. See yourself in action in your mind-movie. For example, if you want a car – see yourself driving it, and then see yourself watching you drive it, adding all the details clear and precise. Be in the drama and in the audience.

If you cannot visualize:

If you are unable to create your mind-movie easily, then it could be that your intuition is telling you that you are heading in the wrong direction. You could be experiencing being guided by your higher self. STOP and rethink what you might be doing wrong or why you are being prevented from creating your desired image. Go back and MEDITATE on it.

Step 5: Add feelings

Now that you 've created a clear structured image in your mind, you need to add a little something extra to it. You need to search for the appropriate feeling or emotion to attach to the scene that you have created. Emotion or feelings mean that you are sensing yourself in the image or movie and this will help your sub-conscious mind, to accept the scene more easily. The sub-conscious mind operates via symbols and pictures, rather than spoken language, and adding a feeling to the image or symbol helps to anchor it. You must be positively sure you know exactly what you want to change and acclimatize yourself to the idea that you have already received it – and how good it makes you feel. Take your time slowly creating the feelings and sensations that are appropriate for the image you are creating. This could be anger or passion, compassion or bliss, love, or joy. Tap into you are your emotional experience and search for the feeling state you require. It could be when you have felt a strong connection or bond with someone, something, an event, or a place. Or it could be a film, play or book that provoked the response you are looking for.

Step 6: Project through your mind and breath

You can use your pattern of breathing to influence ideas towards changing state. In this step, you are acting through the mind and breath and expressing your desired intent onto a physical screen in the material world. The power of breathing should not be taken for granted – it is not just an involuntary action that we have from birth, it is a much more mystical process than we could ever imagine. Breathing not only gives us oxygen but also 'prana' to feed and energize our mind, body, and spirit. All too often we only take short shallow breaths as if we are afraid to breathe, so it is important to learn the right techniques for breathing properly.

How to project your image:

First, think of yourself as a projector. Project the movie in your mind out through the center of your forehead (third eye) onto a screen in front of you. Now imagine that screen is a mirror reflecting back what you are projecting so you can see yourself in action. Next, draw in a long deep breath through your mouth like sucking on a straw. Blow this out slowly onto the mirror at the same time as projecting your movie and 'see' the movie blown onto the screen. You are acting upon the idea you created.

Step 7: Take physical action

You have 'seen' yourself in the image, added the feelings and projected the movie through your breath, the next step is planning how to achieve it. Now that the goal is attracted to your energy, what you need to do is act upon it and observe it becoming a reality. The moment you act upon the idea of its existence it enters your world. Magick requires action to manifest in your reality. As inter-dimensional beings living in the world of spirit first and the physical second, we co-exist in both dimensions all the time. Magick is ever present yet beyond the realms of our perception and reality. It is spirit and consciousness. It is brought into material existence through our mind, body, and action.

It is seemingly impossible to experience the spiritual plane while the mind is consciously active, so dreaming and meditation are powerful tools in magick. Sleep allows us the opportunity to experience ourselves in our most natural state, and because the subconscious mind responds to symbols and pictures, it is the natural medium for receiving messages. These pictures, symbols and unexpressed emotions communicated in a dream state, seem real because you are expressing another aspect of yourself. It is real enough in consciousness, but to experience its reality in the material plane, we must do something to cause it to happen. If no physical action is taken, then the magick remains invisible. Do not wait at the door for your goal to arrive – you need to get out there and actively encourage the goal towards your energy. Mix in the right circles, find like-minded people to mix with, make new and interesting friends. The moment the universe sees you acting it will respond to you.

Next steps

Follow the magickal goal setting strategy, step by step with conviction and dedication and you will easily find your way, to where it is you intend to be. Believe in what you are doing. Be certain of the outcome. And expect to receive.

What Stops the Magick?

- Not listening to your intuition. Ignoring your 'gut feeling' or when you know it just does not feel right but you continue anyway.
- Not believing in you. Kidding you instead of having absolute certainty and confidence beyond doubt.
- Lack of direction. Unclear messages about your desire and intention or constantly changing direction.
- Missing something out of the strategy. Losing focus during the process does not work, it must be well planned, and practiced with dedicated commitment.
- Missing out details in imaging. Not 'seeing' what you want clearly in your mind's eye. You must have precise mental images, not vague images, and scattered thoughts.
- Not forgiving. If you are unable to forgive your own poor choices, and others theirs, you will continue to hold negative patterns that attract more of the same. The simple act of forgiving clears old unwanted emotions, that get in the way of being in control and feeling good about you.
- Attaching the wrong emotion. You must be very precise when attaching an emotion. Be certain of what it is you are trying to attract into your life and what the higher purpose for it is.

- Not decluttering your mind and filling it with good stuff. You need to have composed and positive thoughts that flow constantly, with powerful thinking patterns and clear decided opinions.
- Fully understanding the FOUR ELEMENTS and how to use their symbolism, and function through them, also with them, when certain emotions or expressions are required in a ritual, practice, or routine.

Completion of Rituals

Always finish this way-

By standing upright and turning around a couple of times, then stamp your feet, and clap your hands. Say loudly yes or yippee or hooray or similar and pat yourself on the shoulder. This action will help to anchor the experience, ground your energy, and help you to relate to the world you live in.

- Drink a large glass of water.
- Splash a little water on your face.
- Open a window or door and reconnect to the outside world.
- Keep warm and relax in knowing you are now fully at-one with your higher self as the Magickal you. Now you have completion. So now let go.

Let Go
In knowing the whole thing is done you simply 'let go' of everything you just performed and ritualised. Let nature and the great Cosmic Mind, take its course. Go back to everyday things and simply forget the whole process, as if it were a dream. Because at one time it was. What you have done is 'act out the dream' and causing it to become a reality, in the physical world. Manifesting dreams into Realities.

AND SO, IT IS.

PART TWO

1

THE PLANES OF EXISTENCE

The Planes of Existence
What are the subtle bodies and planes of existence? - There are many versions of potential possibilities and ideas, but in truth, no one really knows the whole mystery or the complete picture. For me, I believe it is part of the wonder and marvel of the whole learning process for each one of us. Physical life in the 3rd dimension is a mysterious magickal journey. Without the mystery or ambiguity there would be no searching for the truth of our own unique creation. If we were the 'reflection' or the 'image' of our creator or creators, then it would have been established in the subtleties' of the elements and energies. Not represented in totality as in the physical material form, or manifestation as a human being. Energy slows down and collapses into form, slowing down to manifest as matter, materialization as a physical entity, yet, continuously aware of itself as pure consciousness. Therefore, everything is energy and consciousness existing in the seen and the unseen world, of all realities. The greater part of us, or the authentic aspect of our being, resides outside of our physical bodies as 'higher consciousness' or higher intelligent thoughts.

Cosmic Mind the Planes of Existence – Here is just one version or an 'idea' but there are many more hypotheses or concepts, look on Google for more information-.

The Physical Plane
Energy is limited to the speed of light. Objects and things are solid. Events are ordered by tine. Space Maintains constant structure. A physical type universe.

The Etheric Plane
Energy is limited to the speed of light. Objects and things are solid. Time is not entirely consistent here. Space is not entirely consistent here. A nonphysical type universe.

The Astral Plane

Energy travels beyond the speed of light but is still limited. Objects and things are NOT solid.

Non-time ordering of events. Events ordered by emotions. Space constantly changes. no consistency. A nonphysical type universe.

The Mental Plane

Energy has no speed limit; it can jump from one place to another. Objects and things do not stay in any one shape or appearance. Non-time ordering of events. Events ordered by concepts.

Space is defined by the distance between concepts. A nonphysical type universe.

The Spirit Plane

Energy has no pattern at all. It can do anything. Objects, people, and things do not exist in form. No time or space ordering. A dimension of the soul, of connections to one another. A nonphysical type universe.

Those potentialities in archetype, fashioned from the spirit of thought. I believe that this plane of existence is the fundamental principle, known as the Holy Spirit or Ghost that is spoken of in the sacred books. Today it is known as 'dark matter' by the scientists... it is the glue that holds everything together...

Kabbalah and Hinduism Thought

There are many ancient spiritual, metaphysical, and hypothetical philosophies, such as Kabbalah, and Hinduism that believe there are multiple realms of existence within the Universe. They accept as true that the Universe was divided into planes of differing existence. Also, that each existence comprising of its own reality, occupied by multitudes of entities, spirits, creatures, and substances. These various ancient tutors, of 'metaphysical consideration' organized these realms, or planes of reality differently, nonetheless they all perceived them as a progression or development, from a lower state of experience, to a higher one. Therefore, the lower planes of existence were perceived as denser, they are more solid, and material. Whereas the higher planes were less condensed, less solid, and less substantial. Hence, they were classified as more refined, imperceptible, and subtle or ethereal, the spirit realms. The ancients intuitively recognized that the universe had countless indistinguishable or invisible corresponding and parallel realities. However, they lacked the science to explain and clarify, just how this was at all possible. This is no longer the situation, there is nothing at all supernatural or mystical about the realms or dimensionalities of existence. Now in modern times, it is proven by science in physics. The nature of physics, conveying those imperceptible realms as energy and frequency. The fashionable phrase that is commonly acknowledged is dimensions or densities. However, it is all one and the same phenomenon or experience as frequency bands. The ancients used the word planes or realms, for these frequency bands and the parallel realities they contain. So, really, we are understanding better the Biblical phrase as The Word or Logos to mean a Sound or Frequency. Energy has no pattern, yet we can comprehend its reality by knowing that Auras and Chakras are existent expressions of same.

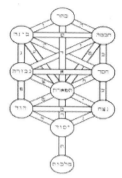

Kabbalah Tree of Life

Expression of Archetype Planes or Realms of Existence
- Google for more information on this subject.

The Inner Planes By-
https://www.dangermouse.net/gurps/demesnes/planes.html

Physical Plane
The Physical Plane (or Material Plane) is that which contains the normal universe, with stars, planets. Most mortal entities are born, live, and die on the physical plane without even knowing there are other planes of existence, let alone interacting with them in any way. It is, however, possible for mortals with the appropriate knowledge or abilities to leave the Physical Plane, travelling through either the Ethereal or Astral Plane, to any of the other planes. Such journeys can be fraught with danger from the physical environments and the denizens of those planes.

Ethereal Plane
The Ethereal Plane suffuses through and touches all parts of the inner planes. Suitable natural or magickal effects can cause material objects or creatures to become ethereal, which causes them to fade from material view. When in an ethereal state, creatures are unable to sense or interact with material objects. They may sense and interact with other ethereal objects, however. Physically, the Ethereal Plane looks like an evenly lit void, in which objects float weightlessly. Creatures can move merely by willing it. In this way, ethereal creatures can travel through the ether to

visit other inner planes, where they materialize if the ethereal state is inactivated. Ethereal travel is generally safe unless hostile ethereal creatures or intelligent beings are encountered.

Plane of Life

The Plane of Life is a place of energy and light. It is a source of tangible goodness and vitality, supplying life force in the form of life-aspect mana to the Physical Plane. Mortal beings who enter this plane can live indefinitely without food or water, although there is little to do here. Undead beings will be destroyed instantly by the overwhelming life force. Native creatures of light and energy exist here and can be summoned on to the Physical Plane.

Plane of Death

The Plane of Death is a place of cold and darkness. It is a source of ultimate evil and decay, draining life from the Physical Plane by supplying it with death-aspect mana. Undead beings have a strong connection with this plane; the magical influences which keep them animated emanate from here. Mortal beings venturing here without magical protection will have the life force sucked out of them rapidly, leaving a lifeless husk floating through the black void. There are some odd native creatures of negative energy who roam the plane.

Plane of Air

This plane is an endless expanse of air, stretching infinitely in all directions. There is no gravity and movement are by physical means such as pushing off other objects or with wings. There are occasional floating lumps of rock, water, and fire which drift through the air, forming homes for the varied creatures of the air which are native to this place. The plane is generally safe for most mortal travelers. It is the source of air-aspect mana on the Physical Plane, and of the air elementals which can be summoned there.

Plane of Earth

This plane is an endless expanse of earth and solid rock, stretching infinitely in all directions. It contains some empty areas filled with air, water, or fire, which form the only reasonably habitable places for mortal visitors from the Physical Plane. Travel is through interconnected tunnels of other material, or by digging. The native creatures can of course move through the solid earth with ease. This plane is the source of earth-aspect mana on the Physical Plane, and of earth elemental beings.

Plane of Fire

This plane is an endless expanse of fire, stretching infinitely in all directions. In some places the endless flames are displaced by lumps of earth or bubbles of water or air. Even these sanctuaries are unbearably hot, however, and any mortal travelers in this realm will need protection. There is no gravity and beings can move by pushing against solid objects or beating wings in the flames. This plane is the source of fire-aspect mana on the Physical Plane, and of the various kinds of fire elementals.

Plane of Water

This plane is an endless expanse of water, stretching infinitely in all directions. Great lumps of rock float amidst this endless sea, as well as bubbles of air and even fire. Air bubbles are the only places an unprotected air-breathing visitor can survive, but the water is not hostile and can be swum through if a method of breathing is available. Water-breathing travelers will be right at home. The plane is the source of water-aspect mana on the Physical Plane, and of water elementals

The Cosmic Mind is Neutral. - It is our consciousness that determines how the Mind expresses itself and manifests in our lives. If we are energy and the Cosmic Mind is energy, that would suggest we are all connected.to each other and to it. In addition to that connection, we have, through our consciousness, access to all the Intelligence, that is the Cosmic Mind. Currently, most people have a poor connection to it because they live in the material and competitive world, with its 'opposition consciousness'.

They have rivalry issues and acknowledge deficiency, as the norm, but it does not have to be that way. They undertake sickness, disease, conflict, anger, and hatred as the general condition of the human experience. However, in the Cosmic Mind, these things never existed. It is our mistaken thoughts and beliefs, that create the reality of the negativizes, as we cause disharmony and disease. Nonetheless, when we begin to cleanse our connection to the Cosmic Mind's energy field, we have a good clear communication. Now that can cause the correct positive thoughts and beliefs, to manifest a more useful and beneficial physical experience

2

THE ELEMENTS AND THEIR SPIRITS

The Elements and their Spirits

Once you accept an alternative concept of the four elements complex ideas become easier to comprehend. Therefore, from this perspective of a magician controlling the elements or wearther, becomes much less esoteric and mysterious.

The Magician Heinrich Cornelius Agrippa 1486-1535

The Elements their qualities and mutual motions There are four Elements as the original foundation of all corporeal things.

Fire, Earth, Water, and Air, of which all element inferior bodies are compounded; not by way of stacking them up together, but by transmutation, and union.

When they are destroyed, they are resolved into Elements. For there is none of the sensible Elements that is pure, but they are more or less mixed, and apt to be changed one into the other: Even as Earth becoming dirty, and being dissolved, becomes Water, and the same being made thick and hard, becomes Earth again; but being evaporated through heat, passes into Air, and that being kindled, passes into Fire, and this being extinguished, returns back again into Air, but being cooled again after its burning, becomes Earth, or Stone, or Sulphur, and this is manifested by Lightening [lightning]: Plato also was of that opinion, that Earth was wholly changeable, and that the rest of the Elements are changed, as into this, so into one another successively. But it is the opinion of the subtler sort of Philosophers, that Earth is not changed, but relented and mixed with other Elements, which do dissolve it, and that it returns into itself again. Now, every one of the Elements hath two specifically qualities, the former whereof it retains as proper to itself, in the other, as a mean, it agrees with that which comes next after it. For Fire is hot and dry, the Earth dry and cold, the Water cold and moist, and the Air moist and hot. And so, after this manner the Elements, according to two contrary qualities, are contrary one to the other, as Fire to Water, and Earth to Air. Moreover, the Elements are upon another account opposite one to the other: For some are heavy, as Earth and Water, and others are light, as Air and Fire. Wherefore the Stoic's called the former passives, but the latter actives. And yet once again Plato distinguished them after another manner, and assigns to every one of them three qualities, viz. to the Fire brightness, thinness, and motion, but to the Earth darkness, thickness, and quietness. And according to these qualities the

Elements of Fire and Earth are contrary. But the other Elements borrow their qualities from these, so that the Air receives two qualities of the Fire, thinness, and motion: and one of the Earths, viz. darkness. In like manner Water receives two qualities of the Earth, darkness, and thickness, and one of Fire, viz. motion. But Fire is twice thinner than Air, thrice more movable, and four times brighter: and the Air is twice more bright, thrice thinner, and four times more moveable then Water. Wherefore Water is twice brighter then Earth, thrice thinner, and four times more movable. As therefore the Fire is to the Air, so Air is to the Water, and Water to the Earth; and again, as the Earth is to the Water, so is the Water to the Air, and the Air to the Fire. And this is the root and foundation of all bodies, natures, virtues, and wonderful works; and he that shall know these qualities of the Elements, and their mixes, shall easily bring to pass such things that are wonderful, and astonishing, and shall be perfect in Magic.

Of a 3-fold Consideration of the Elements.

There are then, as we have said, four Elements, without the perfect knowledge whereof we can affect nothing in Magick. Now each of them is three-fold, that so the number of four may make up the number of twelve; and by passing by the number of seven into the number of ten, there may be a progress to the supreme Unity, upon which all virtue and wonderful operation depends. Of the first Order are the pure Elements, which are neither compounded nor changed, nor admit of motions, but are incorruptible, and not of which, but through which the virtues of all-natural things are brought forth into act. No man is able to declare their virtues, because they can do all things upon all things. He, who is ignorant of these, shall never be able to bring to pass any wonderful matter. Of the second Order are Elements that are compounded, changeable, and impure, yet such as may by art be reduced to their pure simplicity, whose virtue, when they are thus reduced to their simplicity, doth above all things perfect all occult, and common operations of nature: and these are the foundation of the whole natural Magick. Of the third Order are those Elements, which originally and of themselves are not Elements, but are twice compounded, various, and changeable one into the other. They are the infallible Medium, and therefore are called the middle nature, or Soul of the middle nature: Very few there are that understand the deep mysteries thereof. In them is, by means of certain numbers, degrees, and orders, the perfection of every effect in what thing so ever, whether Natural, Celestial, or Super-Celestial; they are full of wonders, and mysteries, and are operative, as in Magick Natural, so Divine: For from these, through them, proceed the bindings, loosing, and transmutations of all things, the knowing and foretelling of things to come, also the driving forth of evil, and the gaining of good spirits. Let no man, therefore, without these three sorts of Elements, and the knowledge thereof, be confident that he is able to work anything in the occult Sciences of Magick, and Nature. But whosoever shall know how to reduce those of one Order, into those of another, impure into pure, Compounded into simple, and shall know how to understand distinctly the nature, virtue, and power of them in number, degrees, and order, without dividing the substance, he shall easily attain to the knowledge, and perfect operation of all-Natural things, and Celestial secrets.

Nothing happens in the magical universe unless someone wills it to happen

-William S Burroughs

The Spirits of the Elements

The Spirits of the Elements
Four Elements as Building Blocks

A Greek philosopher, scientist and healer called Empedocles first described the four elements in the 5th century B.C. when he wrote Tetrasomia, or Doctrine of the Four Elements. He described how all matter was comprised of four elements. His work was in response to the question that philosophers had been working on for many years. What was the universe made of? What was the one element from which it all came? What Empedocles did was question the assumption that it should be just one element. He decided that it could just as well be air, water, and earth. He himself added fire to make it four elements. However, ancient sacred Hebrew idea of the elements as earth, fire and water would mean that air was the bond that held them all together. Later the 4 elements became 5, as the 5th was quintessence, giving rise to awareness as the element of ether. Aristotle later expanded upon the idea and added qualities to these elements, so that fire was hot and fast, air was dry and slow, water was wet and cold.

In the magick of old the four elements are represented as items that you can place on your altar. The 5th Element - To understand the 5th element is to allow the mind to explore the unlimited possibilities and potentialities that exist in the universe. Science calls the 5th element dark matter or dark energy and is only now becoming aware of the reality that it is the 'substance or glue' or as the binding material of all existence. The substance of dark matter or energy and is 90% of all existence and the principle substance dormant in all living things.

Aristotle's understanding of these ideas' dates back thousands of years. He decided upon the addition of the 5th element, believing that it permeates all living things and forms a substance of a heavenly body. We often call this substance the aether, it is this celestial mystery or secret? It is also called Holy Ghost or Spirit. The definition of the 5th element is Quintessence. The word Quintessence and the word Pentecost both have something in common Pentecost is the celebrated day of the descent of the Holy Ghost or Spirit and is represented by a dove. Both Pent and Quint mean 5 or 5th. You could say that 'Space' is the Holy Spirit and pure consciousness. It is therefore consciously aware of itself and encompassing all elements and possibilities for manifestation and materialization.

This idea that we can describe the fundamental nature of everything by reducing it to the elements has influenced philosophy, magick, alchemy and even modern psychology. In the magick of old, the four elements are represented as objects that you place on your altar. Water was represented by a chalice, air by a dagger, earth by a plate and fire by a wand. Once you acquire a clearer understanding of the magickal universe, you will appreciate you do not need a representation of something outside of yourself in order to work the magick. Now the idea of controlling the elements makes a great deal more sense, alongside of the notion of the Great Merlin, summoning up storms and changing the weather. Tarot made good use of personification of them and Sun/Moon energies, as the Universal Law and mans consciousness.

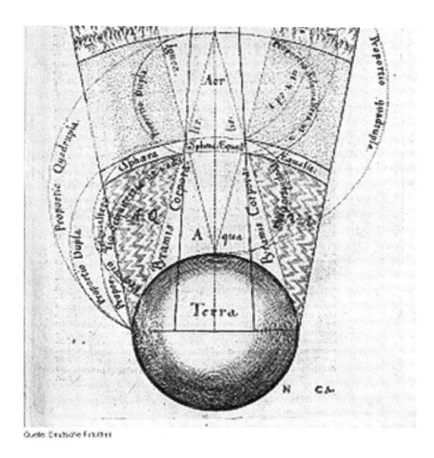

"Imagination is everything, it is the preview of life's coming attractions."
"Nothing Exists in The Universe Without Intention"
-Albert Einstein 1879-1955.

Segment of the macrocosm showing the elemental spheres of terra (earth), aqua (water), aer (air), and ignis (fire), bound by proportional harmonies of the musica mundana (mundane music) Robert Fludd, 1617 (Compare Plato, Timaeus, 32b-c)

The Four Elements in Relation to the Planet

Land/Earth, Sea/Moon, Air/Atmosphere and Fire/Sun

- Earth the power of physical force that holds the atoms together; practical applications; consolidation; materialization. The Earth/Planet
- Water the living soul, emotions; power of the unconscious mind; connecting to source. The moon energies, as ebb and flow of tides, rain. The Sea.
- Air the information necessary for the intellect; the energy that shapes the pattern of things to come power of thought and communication. The Atmosphere.
- Fire the power of directed will; radiating from the very centre of source; the power of action. Divine spark. The Sun.

They are also indicative of the four different directions on the compass. They are more significantly recognized as an intelligent light frequency that governs an element. They are superior vibrations and names in association to the four elements. The Four Spirits who are they? What are their names in scripture?

They are conceded as messengers or angels of the four winds according to scripture. "He maketh his angels' spirits (literally, winds) his ministers a flaming fire" I believe that the four winds carry the elements of creation and therefore, be spirits. From the very beginning of time, the great author of creation expressing his/her consciousness through one imagined contemplation, to differentiate as earth, water, air, and fire, as the one universal law. Expressing four aspects as principles of creation. The four aspects are four elements, epitomizing and exemplifying the physical substance of creative force, and consciousness of the universe. Created as conscious divine beings, or entities/spirits, and given equal authoritative measure of guardianship and governing ability over the universe. Who are they?

They are acknowledged as both The Elements and The Four Archangels? (On the cross of Jesus INRA) coded message as four elements. You could say they are vibratory aspects of the Universe, God, or the Cosmic Mind. They comprise of atmosphere, ambience, sensations, and movement, function, and purpose. They are all degrees of the One Vibration, Cosmic Mind and some people say Sound, Word, or Logos. They are bound or held together by the 5th Element; The Holy Spirit/Ghost is the Holy Ghost the mother of the other four as the Aether?

- Earth – 4th the slowest the vibration it is heavy and closer to material or matter than the others. URIEL.
- Water - 3rd and fluids in the body and all that flow outside. GABRIEL.
- Air - 2nd and finer subtler vibrations held in the air and taken into the body. RAPHAEL.
- Fire - 1st and the fastest electric/fire current inside and outside. MICHAEL.

As aspects of the Father/ God or Cosmic Mind.

Another Idea - https://blog.magick.me/2018/01/25/four-elements/

Fire represents the igniting impulse of thought and of Will. It is the spark of inspiration, the AHA moment. It also represents your fundamental animating life force, the FIRE that causes you to do what you do. When you talk about feeling "fired up," or being creatively "on fire," you are experiencing the element fire in its psychological aspect. This is the element that people often try to overbalance in their psychological make up, and often end up overdoing it. Too much psychological fire can also cause anger, aggravation, and stress; not enough can cause weakness, diffidence, and lack of motivation.

Water represents the receptive impulse of thought. It is your ability to receive inspiration from the universe. It also represents your emotions, and your ability to be in tune with them. Artists and empaths are excellent at working with the element of water: Of creative inspiration, dreams, and emotional intelligence. With the right amount of water element, you can receive great insights into your life, your projects and your relationships (of course, if you don't have enough balance with the fire element, you'll never have the willpower to actually make your great ideas into tangible things!

Air represents the intellect, and reason. It is the logical faculty, the ability of the mind to analyse and reason through situations. This is the element of all great mathematicians, scientists, lawyers, programmers, and anybody else who works with pure intellect. With enough of the air element, you can reason through complex situations that would easily overwhelm others. But too much, and you can easily find yourself in "analysis paralysis," unable to take any actions because you're too caught up in the rational mind. Without enough water—intuition—or fire—willpower—you can easily find yourself lost in your own indecision. But with not enough air, you can have all the willpower and intuition you want, but you could still easily find yourself taking rash and irrational actions!

Earth represents the aspect of mind that is manifested as our own body, and as the physical world. It also represents how we manifest into the physical world. With the right amount of fire (willpower), water (intuition and creative receptivity) and air (reason), you can manifest just about anything into earth (the material world). Therefore, earth classically represents the summation of the prior three elements.

3

UNIVERSAL LAW
THE FOUR ELEMENTS

Universal Law – The Four Elements

The four elements are a formative composition of conception itself and consequently existing within everything, therefore, considered as the fundamental principle and tenet of existence. In the physical world they are the material basis and structure for life and described as the building blocks of the universe. Therefore, this would propose that we could now illustrate the principal nature of everything by reducing it to the four elements. Such is the inspiration it has influenced alchemy, philosophy, magick and modern psychology. So how did the four elements originate, compose, and coordinate themselves, as the original formation and conception, that of pure divine 'Light'?

Science describes them thus-

- Fire- volatile, light, positive electric.
- Air- volatile life energy, positive magnetic.
- Water- condensed life energy, structured energy, and negative energy.
- Earth- mass, matter, dense frozen light, negative magnetic.
-

I consider there's alternative ways to identify with the four elements and how we operate within these realms. I believe we are able to experience aspects of ourselves by simply observing the four elements outside in nature and applying certain principles to effect. Therefore, this interconnectedness can be experienced intentionally. How is this possible? It is possible, when we understand, that we are not separate from the universe, but the microcosmic universe experiencing itself. I see the universe and us as integrated conscious manifestations. The universal intelligence as the Cosmic Mind, as one, and its parts.

Or-

Fire- is the nervous system, neurons that fire in your brain, kundalini serpent energy rising through the chakras, to the pineal gland (3rd eye). The eternal creative source of power, and Divine Will. The sun, lightening, electricity, and flares. Source of Creative Force.

Water- is the sensations, feelings, emotions carried in your tears, sweat, urine, blood, and internal chemicals. The ocean, rivers, rain, snow, hail, clouds, mist. Waters of Life.

Air- is the intellect and inspiration, communication and information that is carried through your breath, and the atmosphere you live in. The essence of life carried in the wind. We connect to everything through air. Breath of Life.

Earth- is the physical material body, stability, balance, connectedness to gravity and being grounded or earthed. We are made of the same minerals as the planet, we cannot be separated from earth, because we are it. Realm of the Physical.

Therefore, the four elements are pure design and principals of creation, they are metaphorically non- representational, yet they are substance and material. Appropriately reflecting a presence in every dimensionality. Spiritual as essence in nature yet they are manifesting through synthesis. By learning to recognize all aspects within us and express our divine essence, and spiritual qualities through the physical form, our thoughts become our deeds and actions in everyday life. Earth as the physical life, is our foundation for expressing and realizing ourselves, through our spiritual principles and philosophy, with a purpose to becoming consciously evolved and embrace elevated ideals. What then are we made of? Spiritual Light energy that condenses to a slower vibration called matter, we are by nature, made up of the entire universe, as the same elements and material through the consciousness of the Creator. There are many ideas and concepts that are connected to The Elements throughout this book; I will mention many of them. However, basically the purpose is for you to really understand the scientific, spiritual, and esoteric idea that brings together the magickal principles of them.

- Fire- The Divine Will.
- Air- Source of Intellect.
- Water-Flow of Emotions.
- Earth- To ground your creative flow.

Fire Element

The Sun - The most obvious representation and worship of fire is the sun, also a source of magnetic fields that reach far out into the solar system. Lightning strikes both follow magnetic fields and create them, dependent upon a wide range of circumstances. In many primitive rituals and ceremonies fires have played an important part of ritual and worship? There is something rather mystical and magickal about an open fire. Watching the flames flicker and dance, can be mesmerizing and soothing to the soul. Recently scientists have discovered that flickering lights, can influence your brain waves, and alter your state of consciousness.

Fire walking is both mysterious and magickal and used in rituals across the planet from Hawaii to Mumbai. It is a highly regarded transition and initiation as a passage of rite. Fire is creative and destructive. It warded off wild animals, intruders, and illness for our ancestors. At a certain point in the combustion reaction, called the ignition point, flames are produced. Flames consist primarily of carbon dioxide, water vapor, oxygen, and nitrogen. Ancient magicians say you will never achieve mastery without the power of fire being present. Ignite the flame within as your passion, and light the fire or flame, as an outward expression.

Magicians and priests used candles to dry out moisture in the air and messages in the atmosphere, in preparation for ritual and ceremony. In Freemasonry, fire is present, for example, during the ceremony of winter solstice, a symbol also of renaissance and energy. Freemasonry takes the ancient symbol meaning of fire to another level, and recognizes that it is destruction and purification, having a double nature as creation 'light' and darkness as destroyer
Fire is one of the four classical elements in ancient Greek philosophy and science. It is both hot and dry, and according to Plato is associated with the tetrahedron platonic solid in archetypical essence. or state.

Air Element

The Wind. - Everyone on the planet is living in the same atmosphere. The messages in the water vapor as air can travel the planet. This atmosphere is made up of mostly nitrogen, oxygen and water vapor and gases. The air that we breathe contains information, so we are breathing in water vapor and moisture. We are also affected by the electrical charge in the air. The ions that are present in the air, also seem to be a vital element in the healthy uptake of vitamins and minerals in our bodies. They affect the release of serotonin, which may cause depression, it can create serenity and calmness too. The positively charged ions that are in the room can be easily felt. Compare that with being in the woods or near a stream. When you start to pay attention to the quality of the air you are breathing you can detect when a storm is coming, or snow is on its way. How cold it is. There is static in the air.

A Great Atmosphere - Even after an event the atmosphere seems to remain, and you can often get a sense of what has happened there. Messages will remain in the air much longer if the atmosphere is moist and damp, foggy or wet, which is why Ireland is such a magickal place.

We give off chemicals through our breath and sweat glands called pheromones. They are most noticeable when we are in an intense state like excitement or fear. You can learn to become aware of the subtle smells, that are associated with different states. We give off different scents depending on our health as well. Diseases can have a distinctive smell and some doctors have incorporated this awareness in their diagnosing. Blowing a kiss. Using your breath to send messages has always been a natural part of Magick. When you blow a kiss, you are sending love and good wishes to someone with the intention of passing good feelings, or to say thank you symbolically, unconsciously you are creating simple Magick. Expressions of emotions move via the fluids in our bodies and are released into the atmosphere through tears, perspiration, and breath, also in extreme emotional disturbances in our urine. We can become overly excited, or fearful and pass urine, as well as nose running and saliva.

Making a Wish - When you blow out candles and make a wish believe it or not you are doing simple Magick. The very fact that you are blowing a message as you put out the candles implies a ritual, with the intent to bring something to you. Wishing is desired concentration and an optimistic outcome. An old method of healing was used by blowing on a soft cloth that is placed over the injured or painful part of the body. This type of healing is remarkably effective it creates warmth with a hidden message passed in the breath.

The air we exhale contains chemicals called pheromones. We expel different pheromones depending on the state we are in; if we are excited or frightened, then other people can detect it unconsciously. Animals are significantly more sensitive to smells than humans are. We are breathing in and out information, in the form of chemicals and water vapor, this influences us and others.

"What is the Universe made of?
What was the one element from which it all came?
Was it, Fire, Air, Water or Earth?

Water Element

H2 O - Water is the most abundant substance on the planet. Two thirds of the surface of the Earth is covered in water and us ourselves, are made up from mostly water. Our bodies are said to be composed of 80% water and the mineral composition of our blood and body fluids reveals a striking similarity to seawater. We gestate in water and can be natural in it and swim instinctively and quite happily when we are first born. We need a regular daily intake of it. It helps aid with digestion and assists to flush out toxins from our body. We can only survive a few days without it, and dehydration is a serious condition that damages our organs.

Healing, Religion and Magick - We have used water for healing and purification for thousands of years. The Romans built spas in many cities all over their empire. Saunas, steam baths, sweat lodges and hot springs are all acknowledged for their healing benefits. Bathing before a ritual is incredibly significant and powerful, you are cleansing your aura and body for the encounter with your higher or Magick You.

Running water is a good example, because it is a great conductor of energy you only need to be next to a fast running river when minerals are present to get an amazing surge, better still stand in it, however water taken from a mineral water spring and bottled does not hold the charge. Water also plays a significant role in religion. Holy water is used during religious ceremonies and plays a major role in christenings and baptisms, and in folklore, we have the Wishing Well. Waterfalls are the most amazing experience for getting a real good zap of negative ions, great for clearing the aura and breathing into your body too.

Earth Element

Carbon - The scientist James Lovelock put forward the idea that the earth behaved like a self-regulating living organism. His Gaia hypothesis was named after the Greek goddess, that personifies the earth. This has been widely accepted by environmentalists although other scientists are less convinced. As well as the two magnetic poles, the earth is vibrating and has its own frequency. Energy flows around and on the planet, through what are known as ley lines and where these ley lines cross or meet, are recognized as important energy centers. Ancient people built their temples on them. The land is not sacred because there is a temple on it; the temple is there because the land is sacred.

We were born to walk with bare feet, not with shoes with rubber soles, that prevent us being able to discharge excessive electricity or to ground/earth it. If we stopped wearing rubber-soled shoes and trainers then we could receive the full amount of electro-magnetic energy we require and begin to feel more connected to our earth. The very fact that electricity flows through our bodies should give us a clue, that we need to be earthed.

Energy Centers - The planet has many of these energy centers, holy places, or sacred sites like Stone Henge. You are part of the earth at the physical level and you can learn to connect with it through balance, resonating with it and tapping into its energy source. You are also influenced at an energetic level by the energy centers of the planet and manmade magnetic fields, from electricity pylons and mobile phone masts. So, learn to feel your feet on the ground and balance your weight, be strong and feel the connection to the planet in a physical manner.

Your Energy System - Just as plants and flowers need sun, water, and minerals from the Earth, so do we. Living plants and animals all possess a quality that has been called their spirit, life force or energy. This is the difference between living and material things, although some cultures have said everything possessed a spirit. The energy system that we possess has been described in detail, by different cultures in India and China. Mother Nature is magnificent, when it comes to giving us exactly what we need to live healthily on the planet. Sadly, we have forgotten to listen and think we know better. All energy is found in nature and in us, it is this energy that makes matter appear to be alive. When this energy ceases to be active in something, it can no longer exist. Smaller energy fields require a constant flow from the larger, if this cannot be maintained they will perish and death must follow, we are inanimate when devoid of energy, life is energy itself. With the fruits this gives us the 'air foods' containing plenty of light and prana or vital energy. Greens and the grasses supply the much-needed water, vegetables that are tubers give us the element of the earth, and grains are the fire elements.

Author James Lovelock- describes the earth as a living organism. So, if the Universe were all mind and intelligence that would indicate that the earth is also alive. Therefore, does it have a consciousness? We are inclined to say the earth is a 'living being' therefore, it would be fair to say 'she', as 'mother' the earth, and therefore, must be conscious of being, and conscious of the Universe that created her. The Universe must have an awareness of its own configuration.

4

THE FOUR ELEMENTS AND YOU

The Four Elements and You –
You will learn – To observe and have resources to tap into.
From – Thinking there is no significant relevance or connection to you as a person and the elements. Seeing them as simply the weather and the planet. The scientific idea of the basic building blocks of creation known as Earth, Water, Air and Fire. Have no relationship to each other. Or they have no other meaning.

To – Experiencing them by observation and sensation to start creating precise images for rituals. Why having a full understanding of them is vital to magickal practices. Seeing how you are connected to the bigger picture and as much a part of the system as the elements themselves. Have resources from experiences that later can be used for rituals or routines. Other viewpoints an esoteric idea and associations to the Mental, Spiritual, Emotional and Physical, alongside of the scientific version. Why you need to consciously interact with both ideas. Observing the verification for yourself.

Exercises and Experiences- Four Elements - Exercises that help to stimulate, enhance, and arouse your imagination. Now you can access that specific energy, to characterize a Spirit and articulate it in a ritual or routine. How do we use the symbolism to enhance what we are doing? By having an experience with the element and then associating it with the appropriate personification of the Spirit of the Element, it can allow a quicker access to that desired state, when we need it. These exercises are designed to allow you a better sympathetic view of how the universe operates and functions. Also, you will soon perceive things you were formerly ignorant of, giving you greater insight on your part in the whole scheme of things. As we are all birthed out of the One Universal Intelligence, as Cosmic Mind, we can operate and function through our 'spiritual essence' to achieve amazing desired results. We cannot disassociate ourselves from the Spirit of the Universe, but we can try this- 'We' can do it, rather than 'I' can do it, so to be conscious of all of your entire being, or 'selves', look at all of the 'you, aspects' in a fundamental and elementary way.

Elements Energy Exercises

Earth Energy –

The planet, our earth is one giant crystal transmitting and receiving messages (energy) via water and electricity (fire) in the air.

The term Earth is used for representing substance, material world, physical plane and earth or ground, as in terra firma. To 'ground' is to earth the electricity that flows through our bodies. When we are unable to do this, we become overloaded with information and energy. It is an essential part of the 'living on earth' experience to ground the creative energy. We must take great care of our mental and physical health, to function appropriately. We must be balanced. Essential preparation to building a stronger physical body is the process of reprogramming the mind. And to necessitate the mind to fully comprehend the nature of balance, strength, stability, and stamina are prerequisites for the exercises you will need to follow. What does this mean? It means they are the fundamental basics, the foundation to all magickal practices. Motion and movement begin in the mind first with ideological concepts that are paramount to activating the physical body. Mind and body are as one, inseparable and dependable upon each other. What do balance, strength, stability and stamina of the mind and physical body mean? Balance is equilibrium, symmetry, parity, and equipoise. It is also composure, confidence, level-headedness, and self-possession. Strength is power, and force or vigor, courage, and effectiveness. Stability is, unswerving, sturdiness and consistency. Stamina is, endurance, fortitude, staunchness, staying power and resilience. However, the physical body remains motionless without the presence of the entity spirit/self. It is a state of dependence in which the significance and existence of the spirit entity is solely dependent on that of another. This is known as 'relativity'.

> *"When forced to summarize the general theory of relativity in one sentence: time and space and gravitation have no separate existence from matter."*
> *-Albert Einstein*

Innate Power Within - You most probably were never fully aware of the physical power that lays dormant, quiescent, and undeveloped. This veiled yet potent living force, constantly available at your command. You may have believed yourself to be weak, feeble, or vulnerable. Or other people may have told you that and you believed them. What can you do about these thoughts and ideas? What principle or tenet needs to be in place, to instigate and initiate messages to the physical body? Simply thoughts. Powerfully charged with conviction, certainty, and passion. What type of thoughts are they? They are positive affirmations designed to convince and promote a new way of thinking about you. What are they?

They are I am, I can, I will, I do. However, magickly it is preferable to state 'We', rather than to 'I' as personality or ego. The practical application of a philosophical thought requires positive inspirations. So, to start the process of clear positive coherent ideas, you require decluttering the old and unwanted, superfluous beliefs. Here is a simple exercise to start with.

Exercise 1

Sit quietly and in a comfortable position hands resting in your lap and take a few deep breaths. Close your eyes and relax. Now begin to remember about all the negative ideas that you had about yourself. Like when you criticize and put yourself down. It maybe for instance, I am too fat or thin, too tall or small too weak, whatever it is that you tell you.

Deep in your sub-conscious you most probably have a recorded message or dialogue that pops into your mind when you are at a low point or unhappy about something. Bring up all of the thoughts that associate with the negative views that you have embedded in your subconscious mind over the years, and those you have absorbed into your subconscious mind through other people's opinions.

Now once you can 'see' the words popping up in your mind's eye begin to erase them one at a time. You can pretend they are words on a blackboard or written on a piece of paper and you are blotting them out, erasing them. As you do this start tapping the side of your temples gently with your fingertips and convince your mind they are gone from your memory permanently. Now take in a deep breath (inspire) and create some positive, powerful ideas about the new you. 'I am balanced, strong, committed and have an abundance of stamina'. Use your own words to phrase it; I am just giving you some ideas. Be sure to visualize the words on your screen in your mind and encourage your senses and feelings to be aroused. Strong and coherent feelings attached to being powerful and creative. Tell yourself it feels so good and you want to remain in that state. Tapping your forehead and temples, as you confirm these feelings and thoughts to your mind. Do this for a few minutes, and rest, take a deep breath. Now anchor the new and positive statements, by pressing the back of your left hand using your thumb in the palm. Press down and think of a trigger word that you can use later to reactivate the state you need. A power word associated to Earth energy, would be a useful idea for example Grounded. Now you can do this procedure, to eliminate any old patterns and fill your mind with fresh new and positive ideas. Remember the power to change exists within you, and it begins in the mind, activates in motion, through the physical body. You create the reality you want to experience. That reality needs to be a state of balance, strength, stability, and stamina. That state is solid grounded and earthed.

Exercise 2

Physical awareness and gravity, balance, and strength, will increase your ability to tap into the energy fields. Begin with developing an awareness of your physical body. Stand in front of a mirror with your legs apart, your arms at your side. Take a good look at you and just be the observer, not judging your shape or size, just being fully aware of the body structure.

Pay attention to your point of gravity, which is just a couple of inches below the naval at the hara point and feel energy, being pulled up from the earth and swirling around at that point. Now imagine yourself anchored to the earth by an invisible chord from the hara point moving down through your body between your legs. Feel connected, stable, and strong as you position and balance yourself to the earth's magnetic field. This will help you to become grounded after working with energy and your exercises; otherwise you can easily become too spacey and fluffy with your head in the clouds. Here is something else you can do to get landed, grounded from the head in the clouds feeling. This works very well at certain times, perhaps when you might feel nervous and feel fidgety. Here is what to do. Imagine you can fly and sense an urgency to return to your place of work, or home. However, you cannot seem to take off. Just take a deep breath through your nostrils and bend your knees, then slowly straighten up. It feels as though you have taken off and left the ground. Now to make sure that you can do it again easily, first close your eyes. Then imagine yourself landing on your feet, landing strong and firm, not wobbly not falling over. Imagine that you have landed and now have 'both feet on the ground.'

This is a physical act of the metaphor we use to describe a more grounded and stable state of mind. Remember, the mind and body are connected.

Grounded- Earthed- You must feel grounded and connected to the earth. When you experience this energy, you are stable and balanced in a physical way, and that allows you to be balanced in other ways too. Good balance is the key to confidence and standing your ground, it also enables you to conjure up vast amounts of good feelings when you need it. Physical awareness and gravity, balance and strength will increase your ability to tap into the energy fields.

Principle GROUNDED AND FEARLESS

- A key to confidence and self-esteem.
- A physical reference for mental balance.
- Part of certainty and conviction.
- Physical power, strength, and stability.

Other Earth Exercises

Take off your shoes and walk barefoot, close your eyes, feel connected. Notice the variance?

Crouch down Indian style, with bare feet, and feel the difference in energy around you, as you get closer to the earth's magnetic field.

Sit on a tiny stool or something wooden just big enough to hold your weight and meditate. Sitting in the traditional style can take your attention away from the exercise. You will get fidgety. The tiny support prevents that, and you are able to absorb the energy more noticeably.

An exercise to try when the weather is warm, is to take your shoes off and lie on the grass with your legs open slightly and palms to the ground. Relax and breathe deeply for a few moments. Look up at the sky and watch the clouds moving (if there is any) or notice birds flying or a plane. Whilst you observe movement and space above be particularly aware of the powerful connectedness to the magnetic earth. Close your eyes for a few moments and see in your mind's eye the clouds, birds or a plane moving across the skyline and at the same time imagine your body merging with the earth below you. For instance, you are a rock and the greater portion of you is connected below the earth's surface. Start to sense the feeling of falling into the earth as your connection to the sky begins to disappear. Remain with that feeling for a few moments and then open your eyes and notice just how difficult it is for you to move. You will be feeling heavy and very grounded. Place your hands on your thighs for a few moments and then with the right hand, hold your left hand and press your thumb into the palm. As you press, take a deep breath, and recall the sinking, falling into the earth sensation, and the idea of being a rock. Release the breath and place your hands back on the ground and then slowly move to stand upright. You can recall this feeling with a trigger word of your choice, example Grounded or Earthed.

Dig a hole in your garden, put your bare feet into it and cover with the earth. Then imagine that you are a tree being planted and visualize your roots coming out of your feet, going down into the ground. Standing upright with your eyes closed begin to imagine the roots searching for water going deeper into the earth.

On a beach you can listen to the waves watch the clouds and imagine yourself sinking into the sand. What can someone do that relates to the earth? Understand Gravity or Magnetism. Walk barefoot might be the easiest experience, since that can represent a big change and different sensation. Picture in your mind, heaps of earth, lumps of clay, muddy land, sandy beaches, crystals, rocks, mountains, landscapes, pyramids rising from the earth or giant obelisks. Visualize sand running through your fingers, holding, and touching stones or pebbles. Walking bare foot in the garden or climbing a hill. Any one of these will give focus to the EARTH energy, that you need to work with. You can imagine lifting heavy weights, do the exercise by using invisible ones and work your way through them, as they get heavier and heavier. Hear rocks falling, or gravel as you walk on it. These are just a few ideas to choose from, nonetheless, do not let that prevent you from creating your own.

What exactly is Earth energy?

- Almost all the energy we have in the earth originates from the sun. Plants and grasses capture the sun through what is called photosynthesis, animals eat the plants, and we eat the animals.
- Coal, oil, peat and gas are all major energies from earth.
- Fossil fuels from animals and plants from millions of years ago.
- Ley lines and electro-magnetic field of gravity.

Hobbies and Activities to Experience

You can begin with doing activities that relate to gaining a sense of balance.

1. Go out for long walks, perhaps on the beach when the weather is fine. Maybe take a brisk walk or jogging, through the woods or out in nature.
2. Hill climbing and hiking are great for strengthening the leg muscles.
3. Try dancing, great for stamina and coordination techniques.
4. Gymnastics could be a way forward, with skills for balance and strength.
5. Any of the martial arts will be useful to you.
6. Roller or ice-skating, snowboarding, and skiing for balance.
7. Handstands and cartwheels are a great fun way to learn a different kind of way to balance your body weight.
8. Help on a farm or conservation work, or land work to connect to being grounded and earthed.
9. Explore caves at the beach or go with a professional group.
10. Sit in a crop circle great for mind, body, and spirit.
11. Going bare foot in the garden.
12. Hug trees and walk in a meadow.
13. Lie in a field with your palms facing the ground and relax.
14. Do some gardening.
15. Collect crystals and minerals.
16. Go on a treasure hunt with metal detector or archaeology dig.

SUMMARY

Earth energy is the feeling of being grounded and connected to the planet. When you experience this energy, you become balanced in every way. The sense of balance is the key to self-confidence, belief and standing your ground; enabling you to conjure up vast amounts of high-quality feelings when necessary. Earth energy is the body called matter in which the spirit resides and allows us to experience the world. We need to ground and earth our creative ideas and thought. We are positive and negative energies that require an earth.

You can also anchor and trigger by doing this- By tapping on the back of your left hand saying a key trigger word when you recall and realize the feelings. Now when you do your exercise just tap your hand to re-activate. Or press your thumb into the palm of your hand, they both work.

5

WATER ENERGY

Water Energy –
Remember those positive times when you felt loved, or, loved someone. When did you feel so good? Perhaps you helped someone for no apparent reason, just because. Was it a random act of kindness or compassion? What about the joy you experienced receiving that unexpected gift? Or the time your heart was bursting with empathy, for a loved one or even a stranger?

You can learn to evoke those moments, which you consider forgotten. Remember the baby in your arms or the sweet little puppy or kitten, so vulnerable and you were so protective? You were allowing love to be present and you were conscious of loving and the feelings it manifested in you. Expressing love is a very innate emotional response.

Heart Zone - Your heart has an intelligence of its own. It is not fooled so easily like the mind. You can convince the mind to do almost anything. You can think 'I feel great' when you feel dreadful. Or 'everything is simply fine' when it's really awful. Your heart will be in pain regardless. Our heart center connects us to the universe, at the necessary level of awareness, to feel the power of the creator within ourselves. The purpose of the following exercises are to build up a strong state associated with love and compassion, and then imagine looping that energy through someone else. To build up a great state, take your time slowly creating the feelings of love.

Blessing Water - Hold the cup or glass in both hands and feel the connection take place between you and your creator via the medium of the water. Say allowed 'divine spirit bless this water' or 'divine spirit of water I am blessed 'or 'I bless the divine spirit in water'. You may use your own words, but something similar will be appropriate. Then blow across the water and say' l am loving you as you are loving me'. So be it. You can blow over it with thoughts that it will heal you, and you are grateful for the healing. Again, finish with so be it or Amen.

Exercise 1

1. You will need to tap into a significant emotional experience that you have had. What you are looking for is a state that you might describe as love, bliss, or passion. It can be where you have felt a strong connection or bond with someone, and that could even be with a pet. You could choose a film; a play or book that you really enjoyed that provoked that response. Just search through your mental filing system for that feeling state, you require its somewhere in your memory.

2. As you start to relive what was happening at the time, what you saw and heard part of that feeling will start to come back, so pay attention to your heart zone. When you find the feeling shine a little bright light on it and let it get brighter and expand on the feeling as it glows and gets bigger and brighter. Soon you will begin to feel the reality of the experience. Now amplify this feeling and visualize the light making a loop, a circle spinning around. Continue to multiply the sensation double it, then double it again.

3. Now the whole loop is a bright pulsating light spinning around inside you, moving around and around your solar plexus and heart zone, creating more and more energy expanding your awareness of the feeling.

The exercise is a powerful and beneficial one, because you will discover an amazing secret about water and how we are all communicating in it all the time. Compassion, loving and caring trigger off the natural flow in the body, to release water or tears. This is a natural cleansing and a healing process. The soul is expressing itself in the physical world.

When other people's experiences affect you, you are causing similar effects in yourself. This might manifest and become a form of healing and divine communication. However, on a negative side it can cause illness, stress, or anxiety if you are in a similar state as the person suffering. Emotions are energy on the move, or information moving out of the body on its way back to source. You will need to tap into this energy for your exercise, so get practicing and remember to choose an in-love state, strong coherent feelings of passion and compassion. Hold onto those feelings and anchor them. By tapping on the back of your left hand saying a key trigger word when you recall and realize the feelings. Now when you do your exercise just tap your hand to re-activate. Drink plenty of water that you have blessed before the experience, this will help to detoxify and cleanse the body ready for communication with your Magickal You. Remember it is essential to empty your bladder before the exercise.

Exercise 2

You are going to connect to your own energy, expand it and create a loop so that you can intensify this healing energy. Then you are going to project that energy out to the person requiring healing or loving energy. Remember everything is already connected; you are purely giving the energy your attention with intent to heal.

1. Close your eyes and place your left hand over your heart and your right over your hara point (just below the naval). Have a clear picture in your mind of mist moving between the two hands and watch it grow and expand.

2. Take a few deep breaths, and in your mind say 'I am healing you with all my love and power' watch the mist move away, and drift off upwards into the sky. It is now a cloud and begins to merge with other clouds.

3. See the cloud over the person, people or place you wish to heal. Take a deep breath in through your nose and blow out the breath as if you are blowing the cloud. Watch as it becomes rain, and it begins to shower down over the person or place. The sun is shining, and you can see a rainbow as it continues to shower fine droplets of rain. Stay in that space for a moment then allow the rain to stop and the sky to clear.

4. Breathe deeply through your nose and slowly exhale through the mouth and in your mind think 'so be it'. Now open your eyes and feel good about what you have done for another. Shake your hands in the air to release the excessive energy. Let the feeling of joy remain but continue with your everyday life.

If you choose to do this exercise daily, choose the same time each day, by doing this you create a ritual, and the power will increase.

Emotional - Energy that relates to our emotions is moving out from the body via water. There is one universal emotion and energy that we call love. Not the head-over-heels romantic notion, but a feeling of complete bliss and unity with the universe. This is the foundation of compassion, sympathy, empathy, understanding and forgiveness. It is how we can see a connection, between every living thing.

- Your emotional brain and chemistry of feelings.
- What determines your behavior.
- One of the keys of the law of attraction or magnetism.

Water Exercises - Water has three states they are liquid, solid or ice and vapours or steam. Take some ice cubes and put them in a saucepan and swirl them around. Listen to the noise they make. Place the pan on the heat and bring to the boil slowly and watch the steam rising. You are witnessing the three states of water.

When it is snowing go outside and hold some snow in your hands and watch it melt. Watch the snowflakes falling and notice that the sound outside appears muffled. Observe the clouds full of rain, and how after a downfall everything seems so fresh and bright... and again things sound different. Go to a sauna and notice how the steam prevents you from breathing properly. Try drinking different types of water like soda, or gassy, spring, or mineral or straight from the tap. You can experiment by drinking less or more water and discover the effect it has on you like dehydration. What difference do you notice?

Water - Imagine water; see in your mind's eye waterfalls, a river, brook, lake, rain, and ocean waves. Sense and smell the sea, salty air, and rain, snow hail, sleet after the storm. Feel water, swimming, paddling, splashing, and rain falling on your face, showering, or bathing. Hear crashing waves, storms, and water running over stones in a brook, rushing rivers, pouring rains. A fountain.

Hobbies and Activities

1. The more you activate the energy of love, healing and compassion the more you will receive back from the universe. Like attracts like.
2. Try voluntary work for sick or disabled people.
3. Work in a charity shop or on a project.
4. Learn the art of being compassionate with yourself and others.
5. Find a way where you can express your compassion towards others.
6. You can begin by simply listening to other problems and try to assist. There are always people in need.
7. Visit the old or help at a youth centre, or similar.
8. Do something charitable.
9. Give something you cherish to someone less fortunate.
10. Organize a charity event,
11. Check on a neighbour or help a stranger.
12. Take someone's dog for a walk.
13. Fundraise, wash cars, water a garden, wash windows.
14. Help out at a hospital or a hospice you will be most welcomed.

Spiritual - is being compassionate.

Physical - Swimming and all water sports.

6

AIR ENERGY

Air Energy –

There are many breathing exercises that will help you to slow down, become more peaceful and lead you into a meditative state. Rhythm breathing that remains slow and steady can help to prevent breathlessness, also helpful with communication, and is beneficial in enhancing your ability to sing and chant. There are times when we all are somewhat inarticulate, tongue-tied, or incoherent and this creates a sense of embarrassment, loss of composure and awkwardness, resulting in confusion. You will avoid these situations when you understand and appreciate these types of breathing methods. You will soon discover that your words will flow with ease, which encourages new verbal skills. Correct breathing will enhance and develop your reading ability too. Studies have shown that children with reading difficulties improved immensely when they learned to breathe correctly. To change your state, you will need to draw in plenty of prana, it carries light into your body. You will easily be able to de-stress yourself; or you will empower yourself and discover much more confidence, assurance, and self-esteem. There are two important things in breathing correctly, inner strength or Ki, Chi, Prana, and a clear unequivocal mind. Combining balance and breathing as an exercise for your magickal practices and experiences you will easily accomplish a great deal. As you progress with breathing exercises it will be noticeable the advantage that you will gain over others in a short space of time. You will discover that you can just tune into these power states, and create absolute confidence, and be convinced and assured that things will manifest for you. You are in harmony with the universe when you are breathing correctly because breath is the very spirit of life. The inherent soul resides in the quintessence of life. The air we breathe.

When you speak you connect to the vapors of source, the essence of life and it is filled with information, that you will in turn breathe in. Always be aware that you are 'creating' each time you verbalize something. Messages on the breath merging with the atmosphere are going to be received by someone, somewhere. Magick is in the air.

What Does Essence Mean? - It means vital, crucial, substantiality, or soul, spirit, and lifeblood. It is the quintessence the essential constituent. What happens when the essence of life no longer resides in the physical body? You are deceased, departed, and dead in body and mind, yet very much a living entity in spirit always without end. Energy cannot die, it only changes form. As a material body returns as dust to dust, or ashes to ashes, so does light return to light, and so is the natural rhythm of life and death, and life returning. Life ever present and never ending, and so spirit carried away on the wind, in the air to return to source having had a human experience.

What is breath? - Inhalation, inspiration, exhalation, vital force.
Transform the way that you breathe, and this will inevitably assist the process of freeing up your mind and transform your thoughts and feelings. Discover how to release negative thoughts and old patterns of belief, through the breath. Inhale pure vital force that is free from your inner chaos and then shift those old habits and patterns onto the out breath. Poor reading has been linked to breathing deficiency If you tend to be short of breath, then you probably have a short attention span also and have difficulty in finishing a task. Many people who get 'out of breath' or 'short winded' also have difficulty in reading. These reading problems can be corrected, just by improving your breathing patterns and posture. Good posture assists your breath to flow smoothly and unhindered. This allows you mind and body to breathe too.

Why we need - Breathing Techniques - There are far too many children that are short of breath or not breathing correctly, which affects their reading ability. They also have great difficulty listening to the end of sentences, and consequently there is a misunderstanding to the meaning, and lose out on learning. Being short of breath also creates the problem of understanding certain levels of perception and thinking. If you are short of breath, then you will have a short span of awareness and have difficulty in communicating with clarity.

Exercise Breathing Techniques

Here are 3 straightforward, 'change of state' breathing techniques.

1. Four-Fold: Inhale through your nose to the count of 4, hold for 4 and exhale through your mouth to 4 make a sound like Haaah.
2. Sanchin: The tip of your tongue pressed up to the roof of your mouth and breathe in through your nose for 3 seconds and out through your mouth for 7 seconds. As you inhale only push your stomach out like a balloon not your chest. As you exhale pull your stomach in and tighten your muscles and imagine gathering energy, at the hara point (2 inches below the naval)
3. Fire/Dragon: inhale and exhale rapidly through the nose 7 times, pause and take a long inhale and exhale to prevent hyperventilation.

More Techniques - Freedom Thinking and Breathing

Let us look at mind/body interplay and what it means to image-up or imagine in your mind's eye as clearly and accurately as you can.

> 1. Imagine you must walk across a narrow swinging bridge, between two mountains and the drop below is hundreds of feet. As you stand at the edge of the drop you look down and all you can see is an endless bottomless pit.
>
> 2. Begin to feel how precarious and perilous the situation appears. Imagine you are about to take the first step, off the ledge, and rocks begin to fall. You can see them tumbling down and down the mountain, but you know you must cross the bridge as soon as possible, because the weather is starting to change, and time is of the essence.
>
> 3. Picture yourself at the edge of the precipice, looking down into the abyss as the bridge begins to creek and sway, as the wind begins to pick up.
>
> 4. Now where in your body can feel the experience and stress?
>
> 5. Now 'let go' of the stress feeling by blowing out a full breath, as if blowing out candles on a cake, and see those feelings evaporate, as a mist leaving the body and going back into the atmosphere.
>
> 6. If you hold on to this 'type' of feeling of fearfulness, apprehension, or hesitation, you will end up spending your life feeling this way. And a possibility of finding other reasons to 'feel' this way, because you have 'locked-in' the feelings from the 'bridge' scenario.
>
> 7. And surprisingly enough, everyone has those fearful hesitant feelings locked into their bodies, from an experience of fear, guilt or physical or mental pain that goes unnoticed. Yet it shapes our lives and even our bodies. It is at an unconscious level, and you need to release the block, to allow yourself a more fulfilling life experience.

We are forever continuing to create situations, of self-fulfilling prophecy, which can produce a variant of other circumstances, that we can easily move beyond.

Freedom Breathing

> 1. Sit quietly in a chair with your back straight and your arms folded in front of you with hands under your armpits. Imagine you are wearing a strait jacket and it is a really a hot sunny day.
>
> 2. Concentrate and imagine how that would feel as it is weighing you down and restricting your movements, as you struggle to get free. Notice how it is preventing you from breathing properly as you try desperately to climb up a hill.
>
> 3. Feel how restricted you are and out of breath, it is just weighing you down more and more and restricting you from moving.

4. But you struggle and struggle to climb to the top of the hill regardless.

5. Now imagine getting free from the heavy straight jacket and make the first breath that you breathe the 'breath of freedom'...Aaahh.

6. And now for the following few minutes, breathe each breath, as if it were that first breath after getting free of that burdensome straight jacket.

7. Now observe the difference and make a comparison, in how you feel, deep within your inner self. Think about whatever the situation was that was restricting you.

8. And now that you have felt some relief with your newfound 'freedom- breathing' pattern this has prepared your automatic system, toward finding relief from it.

9. You anchored the correct pattern for the purpose of creating 'freedom and relief', by simply breathing in response, to the 'imagined' taking off the restricting and burdensome straight jacket.

Whenever you need to experience the sense of 'freedom', simply trigger the situation by thinking up the 'feelings' of freedom, you felt after getting out of the straight jacket and took that first breath. Each time you need to feel free, of whatever it is that causes you to feel restricted, stuck, impeded or simply removing a headache or illness. Use the same system of feeling 'tied-up' and 'restricted' and then released or set free.

Composed Breathing

1. Start by standing with legs shoulder width apart and stretching your arms out. Now begin waving them above your head and all around you. Stamp your feet and clap your hands. Now shake your head quickly and hunch your shoulders as if something creepy has just happened.

2. Now through your nose breathe in very deeply, slowly, taking about 5 or 6 seconds or longer, then exhale through your mouth, very long and slowly, taking 5 or 6 seconds or longer. All one continuous breathing in and breathing out in a perfect rhythm. As you do this feel the ease and relaxation that it gives you. Picture all the stress leaving your body on the out-breath and new life and tranquility on the in-breath.

3. Now breathe in as deeply and slowly as you can, and exhale long and slow through your mouth. Then, on the exhale get your lungs as empty as you possibly can, then imagine blowing out a candle about 18 inches in front of your face.

4. Then continue inhaling and exhaling the breath imagining just who precious and wonderful each breath is, as it flows smoothly in and out. And add more feelings and senses to the breathing. Imagine you can smell the aroma of beautiful flowers. Then at the end of the exhale, try to blow out the candle a little further away each time.

5. Continue this breathing pattern for at least 5 minutes. Then notice its effects on the way you feel, as you maintain this breathing pattern. Continuing a calm breathing pattern, now begin to modify it, with images and feelings of bliss, love, peace, and harmony. Study the changes these images automatically cause in your breathing and in the different ways that you feel.

Enhancing and Improving

Before you take on any major task and especially before any creative work, do a breath exercise several minutes and then go straight immediately to work.

1. You will notice a vast difference in your performance the very first time you do this. The results will seem amazing. Your work moves smoothly and efficiently, no confusion, no hesitations, and practically without error.
2. Each time you do the exercise before any task, it simply gets even better and better.
3. When you are working on important issues that require great concentration and clear thinking, it is paramount to do a 5-minute routine every 30 to 45 minutes.
4. You will be amazed at the results that are achievable.
5. Breathing patterns designed to enhance mind-body-spirit.
6. Continuous deep and slow inhaling and exhaling through the nose, and thinking how smooth and velvety the breath feels, as you inhale slowly.

Breathing each breath as if it were a tremendous relief, from getting out of a strait jacket on a hot day and you can feel the relief... set free to breathe again. Calm and slow breathing with the added images of drawing in air, to various parts where the body has experienced stress or trauma. As you draw in the new clean fresh air, imagine it as swirling clouds, or a mini hurricane that collects and sweeps up all the pain and stress out of your system. When you exhale feel the breath warm and velvety, as it takes all the clutter out with it. The next inhale brings in more clearing and so on...This type of breathing should be used daily to rid the mind and body of old patterns and stress that are deeply rooted.

Sensory Breathing

Is calm and slow breathing and smooth and velvety, with a great emphasis on the anticipation and excitement of what each breath brings in? Try using a real, authentic, or imagined aroma. Breathe the powerful 'sensory aroma' through your nose, long slow deep breaths and send it to every part of your body. You breathe in color too. A great technique to overcome feeling depressed, grief or simply a bit low and sad. It helps to prevent those triggers, that send messages that cause us to feel low. Highly recommend doing daily for 5 minutes. Your breathing creates the 'pulse' for your mind/brain and is the essential key to controlling your levels of awareness and attention span. Scientists have known for decades that poor breathing is associated to reading and language disorders, also attention span disorder.

Feel Good Factor

Feeling good has a profound effect on all levels of awareness, intelligence, creativity, and your performance? Your breathing patterns govern your state, and your state governs your performance. Your intelligence is forever affected by your emotional state and breathing patterns that are associated to it. Probably most of the complications that we encounter throughout life, are self-inflicted by our 'reactions' to situations and circumstance that we choose to experience and then wish at times we had not. You can achieve almost immediate relief from whatever is presently causing you difficulties or bothering you, at an unconscious level.

Action Breathing

For solving problems, feeling less stressed, by whatever is bothering you that seems out of reach. This amazing technique can make any problem or situation appear easier to deal with, simply by setting it to one side. Imagine an empty box or better still have one near you and write down what is bothering you, on a piece of paper then place it in the box and close it. Set it aside out of the way. Now in your mind you can 'put it away,' and simply sit comfortably and keep warm. Begin with long deep breaths, calm breathing, then move to the

Freedom Breathing

Once you are 'set free' from the straight jacket exercise, and the burden of the 'problem' this allows you to see the solution. Or ways to think more positively and feel a solution is now within reach. These routines or exercises can be called a 'ritual'. Freed-Up in mind and body by focused attention to your breathing.

Breath/Prana Energy

Energy is essentially the air that we breathe. It is also known as 'prana' or 'mana' and creates the Ki or Chi energy in the body. It is the essence of life. However, learning to breathe differently and more effectively can have a profound impact on more than just your wellbeing. It is the vital force, or key to life.
- The means to relaxation and energy.
- What determines your vitality.
- One of the keys to healing and magick.
- Primary, connection with higher self and creator.

Air - Get yourself out in the fresh air, sit and breathe by a waterfall. Rejuvenate yourself by spending some of your time in woodland, a forest or near running water. Experience the seaside in winter with a brisk walk along the beach, and really give your lungs a treat. Clear the cobwebs from your mind and start getting new fresh ideas. Inspiration is only a breath away.

Air Exercises- Buy some balloons and blow them up, notice how spacey you get after a few balloons. And how quickly you get exhausted, out of air? Balloons. Release the air onto your face and feel it. Press on one nostril and inhale slowly then press the other to exhale, feel the difference. Left first then right.
Smell something nasty and then something nice...they are both in the air. You cannot observe the wind, but you can watch the trees and plants move. Try to learn to whistle. Copy the Whirling Dervish and stretch out your arms and turn on the spot for a few spins. Feel the energy of air. Get dizzy too. Wave your arms around with your fingers open and observe the energy, then with cupped hands and feel the difference. Huff on a mirror and see the vapor from the air appear. Cup your hand and blow and then inhale through the mouth. Sense the change from hot out breath, to cool in breath.

Hobbies and Activities

1. Swimming and Snorkelling are great ways to enjoy learning to hold your breath.
2. Singing and chanting, the more you practice the better you will become.
3. Yoga pranayama is a wonderful route to spiritual enlightenment, mystical experiences and breathing techniques.
4. Playing musical instruments, wind or brass you will soon learn to hold your breath and make great sounds too.
5. Blowing up balloons for parties or special occasions, is a good way to learn to power blow and exhale the breath.
6. Learn to whistle, it sounds good and you get to control the breath also.
7. Transformation breathing, it is a type of puffing and panting technique that is helpful for releasing negative patterns. Also, a good fast track to higher states of consciousness.

7

FIRE ENERGY

Fire Up –
We have so many hang ups about what others might think or say about our true reactions to a crisis or threatening situation, that very rarely do we let go and be true to ourselves. Many situations have fear attached them, due to the behaviour of our parents or friends, because they have the inability to overcome or fulfil a challenge. Therefore, we are given to believe we cannot achieve our own personal goals either due to their failures. But it does not have to be this way. You can change the old embedded patterning and belief system. How do you do this? By learning new and powerful techniques to overcome fear. How is this possible? It is possible because you learn to personify and impersonate someone great who you most admire. Maybe your hero, sports person, film star or even a cartoon character, it does not matter. What is important is that you create the scene and act the part. You are no longer the weakling or sissy that you have been perceived to be. Now your perspective alters to clear, sharp, and accurate thinking, just like a quick-change artist on stage. Something amazingly powerful has changed in that moment. Performing, the characterization and playing the part of the specific role, you desire to enact. You have changed to a superman or woman, and then back to the everyday life. Now you are fully aware, that at any given moment you can portray and represent whoever you desire to be.

Throughout life we all acquire hang-ups, fears, and phobias, it would seem to be part of the journey. But the journey need not be that way. You could choose the journey of light-heartedness, exuberance and becoming more carefree. But hang-ups prevent the joyful euphoric experiences and are more incomparable to a rucksack full of rock carried around day after day. It weighs you down and becomes an unnecessary burden. The effect can cause displeasure, discontent, animosity, and anger. But, when you deliberately choose to utilize your own unique personalized and idiosyncratic representation, of 'your' hero, freedom abounds.

Soon you will be observing other people's awareness of the new and powerful you emerge, and this will certainly be very encouraging and advantageous.

- From a one thing to another, or transubstantiation as a caterpillar to chrysalis to a beautiful butterfly. The seed of the butterfly is inherent or intrinsic to the caterpillar.

Can you control fear?

Yes, you can control fear before it gives off an odor that other people and animals are able to sense or smell. Pheromones are released through the breath and sweat. What creates fear? You do. You do it with your thoughts, that trigger off a chemical reaction from the brain.

Sometimes fear is created by a conscious embedded suggestion, given by someone else, a situation that you have not experienced before. Fear of the unknown seems to be at a subconscious level and can be triggered by a word or any of the five senses. Another cause of fear manifesting could be when witnessing someone else's reaction, to something they feared, causing you to discover it affects you also. The fears of falling and of loud noises, are the two fears that we are programmed with before birth. Hardwired in our DNA. Phobias create fear, but who or what created the phobia? We are not born with phobias; we seem to attract and collect them throughout life. Babies and young children are devoid of phobias; it is non-existent to the unconscious and learning process. Having never experienced a spider, mouse, or a rat etc., what happens to switch on the phobia in the first place? And what is its origin? Primarily because of the phobias and fears your family express, they get programmed into your innocent mind, and as a child you lack the awareness of a more philosophical outlook, regarding these phobic scenarios. You are stuck with other people's horrors, fears, and strange ideas of what's menacing to them.

Passion -What exactly is Passion? There are different ways to describe passion and to experience it. Passion is intensity, fervor, and vehemence, fire and zest, enthusiasm, and excitement. Passion can be, a fit of anger or temper, frenzy, fury, or eruption. Passion can be a sexual desire, lust, or lasciviousness, infatuation, or adoration. Passion can be fascination, obsession, craze, mania or tempestuous.
So, what if you do not get to experience passion what then? You experience being passive, undemonstrative, aloof, unapproachable, detached, distant or remote, and unfeeling, dull. When experiencing passion through anger you get what is called an adrenalin rush. You start to release chemicals throughout the body, such as pheromones. Blood rushes to the head and you appear 'red' with anger, your temperature is raised, and you feel hot, sweat and shake.
Passionate sexual desire begins at a spiritual level before it stirs the feelings in the body. It manifests outside of our knowing and there are times when the mind seems to be unable to control these desires.
Again, alchemy is working through the mind and body, creating a magnetic attraction in the invisible world, manifesting as desire to unite in the flesh.

Sexual love. There is another kind of sexual/spiritual experience; its created by a commitment to the higher self, through spiritual practices called Kundalini Yoga. There is also Tantra.

What is Kundalini?

Kundalini is a great word but what is it?

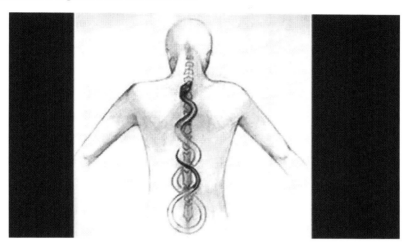

The Sanskrit word Kundalini is quite a metaphoric term the literal translation means "Of spiral nature'. This spiral nature is a double spiral moving up and down the spine or a central axis and has its origins at opposite poles. Also described as the sleeping serpent, that lays dormant at the base of the spine waiting to be awakened. Kundalini is latent or simply embryonic in most people. When aroused it activates an electrical charge or current at the base of the spine the root zone or chakra. And begins the journey upwards. As the Kundalini rises and moves up the spine, it interacts with the other zones, or chakras another Sanskrit metaphorical word meaning "wheel, or you could say spinning energy, or vortices" These wheels or chakras, are energy vortices, connecting our energetic field to our physical bodies and to the universal energy grid. When Kundalini is activated it is an unknown seemingly conscious force, and yet to be experienced or understood by the intellect. It is essential to control this powerful force as the mind and emotions are struggling to understand its purpose and nature. Just as anger requires control, so does the power of the sleeping serpent, the magickal powerful Kundalini energy. It is the hidden, unseen energy, awakened by an inner knowing of its own existence, and presence as the spirit/self. Yet, there is no mystification regarding the awakened Kundalini, however, the outcome leads to a magickal experience.

It would be fair to say here in Western culture, we have great difficulty accepting and putting faith in something non-tangible. We also need perceptible proof that God/Creator exists. Can you not see creation? Take a moment to observe everything around you. We have become victims of our own cynicism, self-doubting and suspicions. Is it at all possible that there is self-will outside of our own thinking? In other words, 'will' or 'will power' as a higher state of consciousness, outside of our intellectual awareness and knowing? Its existence is a reality to its disciples and believers. We need to allow conscious 'will' to avert and prevent the obstacles of intellectualization and have total acceptance of the reality of its existence. Yet the majority deliberately choose not to believe in its existence. Requiring proof. Its simplicity appears too difficult to comprehend, man needs to complicate it. Therefore, we continue to argue the point and choose not to believe in non-tangibility. Santa Claus gets to be real, and self-will and the Creator are questioned as to their substantiality, authenticity, and validity. Believing is 'seeing' not seeing believes, and therefore faith is faith. Yet the sacred books request that we should just accept the reality of all existence. Should we have faith in them or is faith revealed through reading them?

From the Nag Hammadi Library, the Book of Thomas - The Christchrist tells us -"For whoever does not know self, does not know anything, but whoever knows self, already has acquired knowledge about the depth of the universe".

Compare this with a tract from the **Upanishads, the Indian Metaphysical Treatise on Self Realization:** *"It is not by argument that the self is known... Distinguish the self from the body and mind. The self, the atman, the highest refuge of all, pervades the Universe and dwells in the hearts of all. Those who are instructed in the self and who practice constant meditation attain that changeless and self-effulgent atman (spirit/ self). Do thou likewise, for bliss eternal lies before you..."*

"Reality is merely an illusion, albeit a very persistent one"
- Albert Einstein

Exercise 1

You can think about something very powerful that would make your blood boil with passion and imagine it vividly in your mind. Remember the movie you watched, and you felt angry because there was injustice against an innocent person? Activate that feeling. You can easily build a passion 'filing' system full of different scenarios that you have witnessed, but not necessarily had to endure. There are plenty of resources from DVD's and movies. Explore Internet or read a good book for more information. Explore the idea of having a few of the experiences for real and that way, you get to choose what it is you want to use for 'firing up' your passion.

Firing Up - Now you are going to 'fire up,' and this means to raise the body temperature. Start clapping, or rubbing your hands together briskly, and stamp your feet for just a few moments. As you do this begin to pant, breathe very quickly and this will raise the temperature in your body. Concentrate and focus on the type of passion you require for the work you are doing. Angry or Sexual?

Snorting - You take short sharp nasal sniffs to energize adn sharpen the mind. You have got to get some anger from somewhere. Have you ever experienced wanting revenge and did not activate the energy?

How about a situation like your new car just got a bang, or someone just pushed in front of you in a queue and you lost the chance for the last flight. I bet you can summon up a good one if you really dig deep in your history, of horrible moments. Snorting in air very quickly will help to activate chemicals in the brain. You will be able to think more clearly. And act.

Attaching Desire - First thing you need to be able to do is to generate a great state so that you can attach that excitement to your outcome. When you have a desire with a real feel good factor attached to it, it takes you to that place much quicker. You are more easily spurred on to do the things you need to do to get there. With a strong enough desire, you will do whatever it takes, plus this state will affect others when you interact with them and influence the big out there. This is the principle of like attracts like. Others will recognize your energy with similar energy. When you become charismatic, you become magnetic and attract more of the same. If you think 'I wish I could do that,' or have any negative thought or doubts – that puts the fire out. You want to build a rocket of desire. Tap into some exciting, naughty, or challenging experience to stoke the fire. Fan the flames with rhythm and breathing. So that when you think about what you want or need to do then you are turned on by it.

Fire Energy

- Fire up in an instant.
- Create an intense state of passion.
- Project a fire-like energy.
- Feel noticeably confident.

Become Magnetic, Firing Up Intensity of State - If you can stay in the mental state refined as your prime objective until that moment you begin to feel the reality of it, heaven and earth will move all obstacles at will aid in its embodiment. You will always have the innate ability to give unto yourself, that which you are bold and brave enough to appropriate as true. You can satisfy yourself, by saying you are what you want to be simply because others are uncertain of truth. You may be scorned and scoffed at for your determination. But because you set the idea in your mind and by allowing domination of the idea, your ability to bring forth from the unknown will be known. The energy of fire, of thoughts and the sheer overwhelming desire to make it happen.

Fire - Imagine fire, see it in your mind on your screen, glowing flickering see the flames, see a candle flicker, a bonfire and the fire work show, smell the wood burning, the pea or coal glowing. The chestnuts roasting, the barbeque, or sitting around the campfire on a chilly winter's night. Or just sitting by the open fire at home. Feel the warmth on your face, heat from the fire, as you begin to glow. Hear the crackling wood burning etc. smoke rising in the chimney. Thunderbolt, Lightning storms and see camera flashing before you. Incandescent, luminous glowing lights. Fireflies and fluorescent creatures.

Exercises 2

Here is a simple exercise that you can try one evening. If you have not already got some candles, buy some. You will need about 15 - 20. Just make sure they are not scented. Put them together, light and watch them. Notice the effect that it has on your state and your thoughts. In a dark room switch the lights on and off and notice the difference in the atmosphere. Now light candles and do the same thing. But this time when you switch off the lights observe how you feel, with just the candles burning. Notice the difference? Observe the change in atmosphere, not only can you feel heat, but something changes in your state. Sit and stare at them flickering and let your mind drift. When there is a bad aroma light a match...the smell disappears.

Hobbies and Activities

1.   Go to the Gym and really work up a sweat and lose weight in the bargain
2.   Nights of passion with a lover can be recalled when you need to fire up that sexual desire. You are going to get hot and sweat. Breathe faster and hopefully have an orgasm or two. The experience is great stuff to tap into when you need the picture on screen in your mind. Be naughty and have fun.
3.   Get involved in sports, you will soon get fit and strong. You also get to meet people too.
4.   Be competitive and push yourself to the limit.
5.   Run a marathon race; great for group energy and you are going to achieve something incredibly special when you complete it.
6.   Try Kick Boxing it is great for hands and feet coordination and strength.
7.   Any of the Martial Arts are brilliant for fast techniques and powerful rapid movements, building self-confidence too. And Tai Chi for slowing down and focus.
8.   Take up dancing; try Salsa, great for the exercise, coordination and building up a sweat. Its sexy and mixing with the opposite sex, will

be helpful if you are the shy type.

Chemistry

New discoveries about the nature of chemical elements, indicate that there may be more to the ancient description, and that these names of The Elements, are different ways of talking about Carbon, Hydrogen, Oxygen and Nitrogen. There are even indications that the connections go further.

8

EARTH - WATER - AIR - FIRE

Bringing it all together. Again, we need to fully understand what we are doing and why we are doing it. Familiarize with the Elements outside and within ourselves gives a focus of connectedness to everything.

Earth Energy –
You must feel grounded and connected to the earth. When you experience this energy, you are stable and balanced in a physical way, and that allows you to be balanced in other ways too. Good balance is the key to confidence and standing your ground, it also enables you to conjure up vast amounts of good feelings, when you need physical awareness and gravity. Balance and strength will increase your ability to tap into the energy fields

- A key to confidence and self-esteem.
- A physical reference for mental balance.
- Part of certainty and conviction.
- Physical power, strength, and stability.

Principle GROUNDED AND FEARLESS

EARTH – Balance - You will learn from –
- Poor posture and poise.
- Lazy and tired.
- Unstable on your feet.
- Weak at the knees.
- Ungrounded.
- Clumsy.
- Awkward and self-conscious.

To -
- Move and hold your posture, poise, and presence.

- Aware of your physical strength, coordination, stability, and balance.
- Fitter and more energized.
- Aware of connection to gravity, grounded or earthed.
- Help to breathe correctly.
- Help with digestive system
- Feel connected to the earth's magnetic field.
- Relax more easily.
- Be more expressive and physically aware.
- Agile and lively.

Water Energy –

Energy that relates to our emotions, it is moving out from the body via water. There is one universal emotion and energy that we call love. Not the head-over-heels romantic notion, but a feeling of complete bliss and unity with the universe. This is the foundation of compassion, forgiveness and how we can see a connection between us all.

1. Your emotional brain and chemistry of feelings.
2. What determines your behavior.
3. One of the keys of the law of attraction.
4. Empathy, Sympathy and Compassion

Principle SENSATIONS and CONNECTEDNESS

WATER- Flow of Emotions - You will learn from –
- Over emotional.
- Lack compassion.
- Overreact.
- Depressed.
- Affected easily by other emotions.
- Too weepy.
- Too hysterical.
- Unable to connect to others pain.
- Unsure of your feelings.
- Unable to tap into past experiences and let them go.
- Self-destructive.

To –
- Inner peace and balance.
- Directed energy to emotional states.
- Controlled emotions.
- Connected to higher feelings and senses.
- Expressing joy, excitement, passion, and love.
- More compassionate to others and yourself.
- Able to express what you feel.

- Feel differently towards others.
- Rapport with others.
- Stronger intuitively.
- Express your higher self.
- Learn to love.

Air Energy –

Energy is essentially the air that we breathe. It is also known as 'prana' or 'mana' and creates the ki or chi energy, in the body. It is the essence of life. However, learning to breathe differently and more effectively can have a profound impact on more than just your well-being. It is the vital force, or key to life.

- The means to relaxation and energy.
- What determines your vitality.
- One of the keys to healing and magick.
- Primary, connection with higher self and creator.

Principle COMMUNICATION and VITAL FORCE

AIR – Breathing - You will learn from –

- Shallow, ineffective breathing that is just enough to keep you alive.
- Unable to concentrate.
- Get out of breath quickly.
- Fatigue and lethargy.
- Lack vital energy.
- Cannot think clearly.
- Lack communication.
- Devoid of energy.

To –

- Powerful deep breathing.
- Fully awake and energized.
- Snort to activate energy
- Able to meditate and relax.
- Help you to concentrate.
- Help you to sleep better.
- Focus on your feelings
- Oxygenate your entire body.

Fire Energy –

Energize in a very intense and expressive way through anger or passion. You can experience this intensity and how to tap into it, in an instant. What happens when you experience this energy?

- Fire up in an instant.
- Create an intense state of passion.
- Project a fire-like energy.
- Feel noticeably confident.
- Become magnetic.

Principle PASSIONATE and POWERFUL

FIRE– Firing Up - You will learn from –
- Negative thoughts.
- Vague mental images.
- Tangled cluttered thoughts.
- No disciplined thinking.
- Constantly changing direction.
- Unclear mental concepts.
- Having difficulty with decision-making.
- Holding onto old patterns.
- Lack mental power.
- Slow to act.
- Uncontrolled mental energy.
- Dull and uninteresting
- Low self-esteem and negative thinking.
- Confused.
- Fear.
- Uncertain.

To –

- Focused energy.
- Clear positive thinking.
- Take Action.
- Certainty.
- Be magnetic and charismatic.
- Dynamic and have authority.
- Look vibrant and radiant.
- Confident and positive.
- Passionate.
- The master of your destiny.
- Positive and detailed mental images.
- New and powerful thinking patterns.
- Decided opinions.
- Specific authoritative commands.

Understanding now that you are these Elements, they are outside and inside of you. Having a reference to create your ritual, routine with will enable a greater sense of connectedness to everything. You are consciously communicating with Cosmic Mind and the Universal Laws.

9

7 STEPS TO MAGICK

7 Steps to Magick- Ritual- Routine-Exercise –
Let us take another look at it all again- Remember to attach the correct Element/ or Elements to your ritual/routine. It is always about the state you are in that determines the outcome. So, Let us Take A Closer Look at Air and Breathing FIRST. Various experiences cause a variety of breathing patterns and different types of breathing can be used to predispose, a range of experiences, that we might be having. You can consciously use your pattern of breathing to influence your thoughts

1. Understand insights.
2. Self-acceptance.
3. Creative ability.
4. Problem solving.
5. Health issues.
6. Changing state.
7. Higher levels of awareness.

What else is so important about the way we breathe? Poor reading has been linked to breathing deficiency. Scientists inform us that poor breathing is associated to reading, language and attention span disorders. When you breathe shallow or you are 'short of breath' you have a short attention span and difficulty in finishing a task. This may cause the inability to concentrate and 'listen' and 'understand' the end of sentences. Reading problems can easily be corrected by improving your breathing patterns and posture. Good posture assists your breath to flow smoothly and unhindered. This allows you mind and body to become energized or relaxed and therefore more balanced.

People are often classed or categorized as 'dyslexic' when in fact it is simply a case of 'poor breathing habits'. Poor and lazy breathing habits can cause a lack of understanding, in certain levels of perception, and clear-thinking ability. How often have you heard?

"I can't think straight, I need some fresh air".

Breathing Patterns Designed to Enhance Mind-Body-Spirit
1. Continuous deep and slow inhaling and exhaling through the nose, and thinking how smooth and velvety the breath feels, as you inhale slowly.
2. Breathing each breath as if it were a tremendous relief from getting out of a strait jacket on a hot day and you can feel the relief to be set free to breathe again.
3. Calm and slow breathing with the added images of drawing in air to various parts where the body has experienced stress or trauma. As you draw in the new clean fresh air imagine it as swirling clouds, or a mini hurricane that collects and sweeps up all the pain and stress out of your system. When you exhale feel the breath, it takes all the clutter out with it. And the next inhale brings in more clearing.

When you are calm breathing, pain, distress, or any other 'disturbing' emotions cannot co-exist for very long in the same 'psychological space'. Your breathing continues, long after the cause of distress has shifted. And believe it or not it soon goes. Using a magickal breath language, you can easily change your 'physiological state' also you can easily combine this breath language, with a 'method' of' walking and thinking' to change old patterns and habits. Calm breathing should be practiced daily to rid the mind/body of old patterns and stress that are deeply rooted and to overcome feeling depressed, grief or simply a bit low or sad. It helps to prevent those 'triggers' that send the messages in the first place. Therefore, breathing correctly creates the 'pulse' or 'rhythm' necessary for the mind/brain, and is essential to all levels of awareness and attention span.

To Begin a Routine or Ritual -Unzipping Your Energy Field –

We begin the process of entering 'sacred space' and getting into your Magick circle/bubble. So, stepping into your circle/bubble, the first process you are going to do is known as unzipping. Using your right hand, just below your bottom lip, run your hand swiftly down the front of your body about a few inches away, as it leaves the bottom lip making a downward stroke. This is opening the chakras for you to begin the process. Now you are unzipped and open to the elements, or the four energies, and to all energy fields, so you need to have clear thinking. There are four energies that you are working with, they are fire, water, air, and earth. Remember, all messages are contained in the air we breathe...they move about via the wind and rain, but require the energy of the sun, fire, and electricity to be creative within our minds. All contained in a physical earthly body.

Everything is Unfolding - Energy is collapsing into realities, that are held together by the power of our thoughts. It is through the process of desired intention, and awareness of consciousness, that we can 'Will' things into existence. You are observing the universe with every thought; you are the 'creator' of everything that you choose to experience. That's Magick!

Magick Keys - What are the fundamental principles of Magick? What is the basic groundwork that is necessary to achieve positive results?

- Know exactly what you want.
- Create a state of confidence and certainty.
- Form new patterns of thought that will influence.
- Provoke a change of state in the mind.
- Integrate mind and body.

As a Warning - It is vital to be in control of yourself first before you ever attempt to Magick up your hidden powers. If you cannot control yourself, your emotions, anger, or passion in this world, then you haven't a hope of controlling the Magickal you, once it's set free. Once you let the Genii out of the bottle. Sometimes I have made that fatal error and ended up back where I started. Concentration is just one of the keys.

Nothing happens in the universe without intent, so before you begin there must be in place your intentional desire. Once you have that fixed in your mind then the basic steps are relatively easy, yet powerful. Hold the vision.

1. Control your physical body- balance and grounded.
2. Control your emotions- connectedness and coordinated.
3. Control your breathing- energize and relax.
4. Control your mind- concentration and focus.

You need to feel connected to the world that you live in, before attempting to enter the world of the spirit. You need to feel grounded and aware of your physicality. Start by being aware of your body size and weight. This does not mean jumping on the scales it means feeling your body size and balancing your weight. Every good building needs a strong solid foundation. So, you start there. Shoes off and recharge with the electro- magnetic earth energy, stand strong and firm, grounded.

Because - You will need to get used to the feeling of being grounded and connected to the earth. When you experience this energy, you are stable and balanced in a physical way and that allows you to be balanced in other ways too. Good balance is the key to confidence and standing your ground, it also enables you to conjure up vast amounts of good feelings, when you need it. You need to be in total control of your emotions and feel centred and composed too.

Because If you lose control of your emotions you are likely to be in a weak or vulnerable state. You will need to learn to detach yourself from your personal involvement, in certain situations, especially the outcome of your intent. Emotions play a big part in healing and when you switch on to the compassionate feelings you need to separate your own emotions, from that of the person you are healing. You can easily be affected mentally and physically and take on their pain too. Emotions play a big part in how you feel about yourself. In Magick you need to disassociate, as quickly as you recall the feeling. You must be able to breathe correctly it helps you to energize and relax too.

Because - If you are in a panic you simply lose your ability to breathe correctly. The air we breathe contains information on many levels. When we are in certain states, we may have rapid or unsystematic breathing patterns, we need to have breath deeper and calmer. Using breath to send messages, has always been a major part of Magick. Your mind believes that it governs you, now is the time to control it of its constant idle chatter. The air you breathe out contains information in the form of chemicals that relate to your physiological state. In Magick, that state is influenced by your intention.

Preparation-

1. **Desire-** you must be positive about what you want. There must be genuine deep emotions and feelings attached to the desire. And a clear picture in your mind, of what or how, it looks and feels and smells etc.
2. **Clear Mind-** you need to have clear and positive statements, concerning the way you programmed your mind, to believe the desires are certain of arriving. Structure and anchor suggestions, that you can tap into.
3. **Focus and Intention-** means that for days before you act with body movements, as the act of the ritual, you are convincing yourself of the arrival and positive outcome. Your intention is receiving.

Basic Principles of Magick in Action.

- Desire, Aspiration or Request, must be clear and precise.
- Intent, Purpose or Goal, must have a direction.
- Create Sacred Space, circle / bubble, must feel safe to work in.

OPEN UNZIP YOUR AURA AND CHAKRAS
- Balance the energy fields, as the elements, must apply the forces in nature to assist and control the outcome.
- Empty the mind of clutter and chatter, must have clear positive thoughts.
- Balance the mind, focus on certainty or your desire, must bring it all together.
- Balance the body, feel balanced, strong, and commanding, must be certain and grateful.
- Focus the Intent and breathe deeply in rhythm, must flow with the forces in nature.
- Say Magickal words gibberish or nonsense, must allow the mind to drop its chatter, gibberish allows the mind to empty and receive Light to the pineal gland, 3rd eye. See the Desire on Screen
- Wave your arms around, must create energy by activating the aura and chakras for maximum electricity to attract your Desire.

- Blow the Magick into the room, must send the desire out on the breath into the positive active atmosphere.
- Relax.
- Give thanks, So Be It or Amen

CLOSE ZIP UP YOUR AURA AND CHAKRAS

'A Consequential Outcome'

Focused or Conscious Breathing, Gratitude for what you are about to receive, feel deeply appreciative for what you manifest, and the universe will constantly reward you. The Universe will eternally reward you, with that which you claim is true of yourself. The Universe does not care whether you call yourself rich or poor. It loves you and will support your every belief and gives you more of that, so stop asking yourself whether you are worthy or unworthy to receive that which you deserve. A template of desire is fashioned by what you believe yourself to be. It is self-realized, not yourself as John Smith or Anne Brown, but the higher Magickal You, yet it is all one and the same self. It is your very being as the consciousness of that fact, it is heaven, space, and spirit. Understand this, you think you created a desire, your desires are ever fashioned within you simply because of whom you claim yourself to be.

The conscious mind understands mesmerism; however, it cannot be hypnotized under the influence of suggestion, the sub-consciousness being the illogical to a large degree, will willingly accept and react to suggestions. So, is that not an invitation for you to suggest something to your subconscious mind, to get in touch with Magickal You. The subject matters not, what does matter, is your subconscious will react to your suggestions. You are in Command of it. Hypnosis stems from the innate power to control others, to control by hypnosis is tapping into and using the vital force, the magnetic response, the forces in nature. It is the spirit of the subconscious that controls those fine threads, all that marvelous shadowy body, the substance that carries and moves through the thought forms, after the thinking process is done. And it also has control of all the bodies' electric currents. Magick is about sending messages as thought forms to the subconscious, to be given to the conscious self in due time. All prayer is telepathic. We cannot sense and receive telepathic messages at will, it is most necessary to give a clear mental image, or order, for the subconscious to transmit and receive. All we must do, is to sit back and relax in the knowing that it is happening. This is a process, which is like; waiting for all those forgotten memories to pop up again, you know, it is there for certain and it will reveal itself sooner or later. Always remember there is a higher order to the universe, and that order can be influenced.

Each of us in humanity are instruments of God as Cosmic Mind; we all have our own sound as vibration. The sound you create is just one in the great orchestra of sounds, of octaves. When unwell, you are as violins out of tune, when in perfect health you are finely tuned, a reverberating instrument in the great orchestra.

You are a body of light as 'Spirit', resonating at 350.000 to 450.000 light waves per second. When your physical life ceases to be, your light or spirit returns to source, to the universe or matrix. As your earth body returns to source, back to earth. You have experienced a human reality, through the encounters chosen by you. Then back to your original self, and where you came via the Cosmic Consciousness Mind, the universal grid. Light is pure energy, it never ceases to be, and it just is, through the great network of the eternal essence or source. Whilst we are here in the third dimension, in the physical world, we are inter-dimensional beings, through the light body and high consciousness. We are consciously aware in dream state and in active state, yet our physical bodies are like lampshades, never revealing its authentic reality. However, the more consciously aware we become, the more radiant we are and develop more power for attracting magickal experiences to our reality.

Miracles and Magick, occur in the mastery of knowing the master creates the day, with unlimited mind, does not allow the day to create him. He controls his mind; he does not allow his mind to think that it is in control of him.

There is only one true language in the universe: it is the Language of Light. When man begins to discover that he is the creator of his own reality, he can then transcend from the nature of existence, as a human being, to the authentic divine reality of light. We move away from animal instinct, to the high frequencies of the Creator, the Cosmic Mind. Firstly, we must stop blaming others for our mistakes, and be responsible for our own actions. The most powerful way to share this light and become radiant, is to share this knowledge and to live it. Become it.

For more information on energy fields, universal laws, and our part in it, I have written- 11:11 Language of Light

Completion of Rituals - Always finish this way-
By standing upright and turning around a couple of times, then stamp your feet, and clap your hands. Say loudly yes or yippee, or hooray or similar and pat yourself on the shoulder. This action will help to anchor the experience, ground your energy, and help you to relate to the world you live in.

- Drink a large glass of water.
- Splash a little water on your face.
- Open a window or door and reconnect to the outside world.
- Keep warm and relax, in knowing you are now fully at-one with your higher self as the Magickal You. Now you have completion. So now let go.

Let Go Means - In knowing the whole thing is done you simply 'let go' of everything you just performed and ritualised. Let nature and the great Cosmic Mind, take its course. Go back to everyday things and simply forget the whole process, as if it were a dream. Because at one time it was. What you have done is 'act out the dream' and causing it to become a reality, in the physical world. Manifesting dreams into realities using the forces in nature, your mind and connecting with the Cosmic Mind.

You can easily create another wish or desire and put into effect its manifesting into your world. The more you practice the stronger the signal and the quicker the results. And So, It Is...

Remember you can work your Magick Rituals in the day for SUN/ Fire/Male energies, and at night for MOON/Water Air/Female.
-Earth Your Creative Influence-
Connect with The Cosmic Mind

"I am no longer cursed by poverty because I took possession of my own mind, and that mind has yielded me every material thing I want, and much more than I need.
But this power of mind is a universal one, available to the humblest person as it is to the greatest"

-Andrew Carnegie

Other Titles by Barony Books including this Author

Front Cover Design without text will be available soon on posters and T-shirts.

Email Barony books at
https://www.baronybooks.com
for distribution link.

INDEX

NOTES

NOTES

Printed in Poland
by Amazon Fulfillment
Poland Sp. z o.o., Wrocław

24197221R00097